WAGING
PEACE

WAGING PEACE

A SPECIAL OPERATIONS TEAM'S
BATTLE TO REBUILD IRAQ

ROB SCHULTHEIS

GOTHAM BOOKS

GOTHAM BOOKS
Published by Penguin Group (USA) Inc.
375 Hudson Street, New York, New York 10014, U.S.A.
Penguin Group (Canada), 10 Alcorn Avenue, Toronto, Ontario, Canada M4V 3B2 (a division of Pearson Penguin Canada Inc.); Penguin Books Ltd, 80 Strand, London WC2R 0RL, England; Penguin Ireland, 25 St Stephen's Green, Dublin 2, Ireland (a division of Penguin Books Ltd); Penguin Group (Australia), 250 Camberwell Road, Camberwell, Victoria 3124, Australia (a division of Pearson Australia Group Pty Ltd); Penguin Books India Pvt Ltd, 11 Community Centre, Panchsheel Park, New Delhi - 110 017, India; Penguin Group (NZ), cnr Airborne and Rosedale Roads, Albany, Auckland 1310, New Zealand (a division of Pearson New Zealand Ltd); Penguin Books (South Africa) (Pty) Ltd, 24 Sturdee Avenue, Rosebank, Johannesburg 2196, South Africa

Penguin Books Ltd, Registered Offices: 80 Strand, London WC2R 0RL, England

Published by Gotham Books, a division of Penguin Group (USA) Inc.

First printing, June 2005
10 9 8 7 6 5 4 3 2 1

Copyright © 2005 by Rob Schultheis
All rights reserved

Gotham Books and the skyscraper logo are trademarks of Penguin Group (USA) Inc.

LIBRARY OF CONGRESS CATALOGING-IN-PUBLICATION DATA
has been applied for.

ISBN 1-592-40127-9

Printed in the United States of America
Set in Bulmer MT
Designed by Elke Sigal

For the men and women of Civil Affairs Team 13, Alpha Company,
the 425th CA Battalion (Reserve);
for the troops of the 1/5 Cav, the "Black Knights";
and for all the soldiers of USACAPOC
who have given their lives serving their country
and the people of Iraq

"Win the war, and also win the peace."

—*Gen. George Patton*

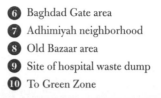
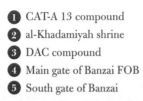

1. CAT-A 13 compound
2. al-Khadamiyah shrine
3. DAC compound
4. Main gate of Banzai FOB
5. South gate of Banzai

6. Baghdad Gate area
7. Adhimiyah neighborhood
8. Old Bazaar area
9. Site of hospital waste dump
10. To Green Zone

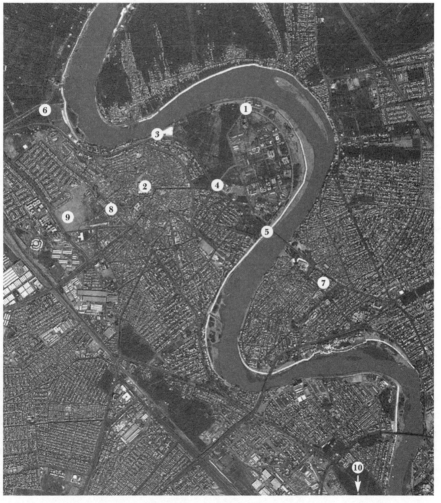

Satellite image courtesy of Digital Globe

MAP OF AL-KHADAMIYAH

GLOSSARY

ALI BABA GI/Iraqi slang for thieves or "bad guys."

A-LOC Headquarters of Alpha Company.

AO Area of Operations of a military unit. The 425th CA Battalion's AO covered most of western Baghdad and the surrounding countryside, while the AO of Civil Affairs Team 13 of the 425's Alpha Company was the al-Khadimiyah neighborhood of northwestern Baghdad.

BA'ATH PARTY Originally a legitimate pan-nationalist socialist political party in Syria, Iraq and other Middle Eastern countries; in Iraq under Sadam Hussein it became a Mafia-style regime whose authority permeated every area of life.

BIAP Pronounced "Bye-ap." Baghdad International Airport.

BOHICA Army slang for "Bend Over, Here It Comes Again."

"BRAGG" Short for Fort Bragg, headquarters of the 82nd Airborne Division, most of the Army's Special Forces units, and

USACAPOC (A) (see below). Located in Fayetteville, North Carolina, jocularly known as "Fayettenam."

CAT Civil Affairs Team, usually consisting of seven or eight soldiers, and usually assigned to its own AO, where it carries out a wide range of aid missions. The team I was with in Iraq was CAT-A 13—Civil Affairs Team 13 of Alpha Company, the 425th CA Battalion.

CO Commanding Officer. The highest ranking member and ultimately the boss of a military unit.

CPA Coalition Provisional Authority. The first occupation governing body in postwar Iraq, headed by Paul Bremer. In the summer of 2004 it gave way to the Iraqi Interim Government.

DAC District Advisory Council. Popular Iraqi representative bodies, organized and encouraged by the U.S., that help local citizens make municipal policy and get aid projects started in their areas. Members include tribal sheikhs, religious leaders, businessmen, and even outspoken critics of the U.S. occupation. Below the DACs are smaller, more localized NACs, or Neighborhood Advisory Councils. In Baghdad, the DACs have representatives on the Baghdad City Council.

DFAC "Dining Facility" in Army acronym lingo.

FOB Forward Operating Base, sometimes known as Forward Patrol Base. Many Army units in Iraq operate out of FOBs, which are scattered across the country. CAT-A 13 was based at

Banzai FOB, along with the 1/5 Cav Battalion, in northwest Baghdad. Many FOBs were much smaller and manned by fewer troops. Some, like Anaconda and Dagger, were notoriously dangerous, surrounded by hostile locals, and so small in area that almost any rocket or mortar shell hitting them had a good chance of inflicting casualties.

GREEN ZONE The highly fortified area of downtown Baghdad, on the west bank of the Tigris, where the U.S. occupation and Interim Government are based. Formerly the inner sanctum of Saddam and his Ba'ath Party cronies. Many Iraqis have criticized the United States for moving into the palaces and offices of the old dictatorial regime. With its wealthy contractors cruising in brand-new SUVs and Beltway carpetbaggers living in mansions with lawns and swimming pools, the Green Zone is the target of frequent derisive joking from GIs.

HAJJI U.S. Army slang for "Iraqi." In Arabic, it is an honorific term for someone who has completed the *hajj,* or pilgrimage, to Mecca. In occupied Iraq, it has become an all-purpose adjective: locally made mattresses are "hajji pads," Iraqi-owned stores on U.S. posts are "hajji shops," and so on.

IED Improvised Explosive Device, the main weapon of the Iraqi resistance. Usually composed of mortar rounds, artillery shells or rockets, camouflaged as roadside debris and set off by remote control using cell phones or garage door openers. Now the insurgents are also using VIEDs, or Vehicular Improvised Explosive Devices, explosives-rigged vehicles either driven by suicide drivers or parked and set off by remote control.

INDIGS Army slang for local people, usually referring to those fighting on our side as irregulars. Dates back to Vietnam, where Nungs, Montagnards, ethnic Cambodians and other Vietnamese minorities were recruited into platoon-, company- and battalion-sized forces often led by U.S. Special Forces NCOs.

INGs Iraqi National Guards. This newly recruited force has had a mixed record so far, sometimes performing well, but more often not, when confronted with insurgent forces.

IP Iraqi Police. Not trusted by either Iraqis or U.S. troops. Frequently crooked, or working for whoever pays them the most. They have improved in recent months.

"IRENE" Army radio code word for "Emergency! Get out of here, fast!" Unique to Iraq, to the best of my knowledge.

KEVLAR Synonym for regulation Army helmet; named after the ballistic (bullet-resistant) material the helmet is made of. American body armor was also made of Kevlar until recently, when a new improved material was introduced.

KILO INDIA ALPHA Radio shorthand for "Killed in action."

MEDCAP A temporary medical mission for civilians, set up by the military.

NGO Non-Governmental Organization. Refers specifically to foreign aid groups, such as Medicins Sans Frontiers ("Doctors Without Borders") and Save the Children, not supported by the

United Nations or national governments. The lack of NGOs in Iraq due to the ongoing violence has put an overwhelming burden on the Army's Civil Affairs teams.

OD Olive Drab, the traditional hue all Army property was once painted in. Also a synonym for someone or something "100 percent Army."

Opcon Civil Affairs teams in the field are "opconned," placed under the command and control of the major combat arms unit in the area: in Baghdad, this was either the 1st Armored Division or the 1st Cavalry Division. Traditionally, CA units are supposed to do only what the combat arms CO tells them, which can be extremely dysfunctional; some "gunslinger" COs in Iraq, who didn't believe that nation-building and aid work were "soldierly," had the CA units in their area pulling night patrol and anti-insurgent sweeps. This was a problem in all of Iraq, as the generals running the war out of Baghdad consistently refused to allow Civil Affairs officers the autonomy necessary to "do their thing."

OPSEC Operational security: radio call signs, codes, convoy routes, troop rotations, weapons status—anything that if known by the enemy would endanger U.S. troops in the field—is covered by OPSEC rules, i.e. kept under wraps.

REMF Army slang for "Rear Echelon Motherfucker," a disparaging term for those not on the front lines.

RPG Rocket-Propelled Grenade. A misnomer, as it actually refers to a small shoulder-fired rocket whose warhead is not a grenade but a much larger anti-armor, antipersonnel, or incendiary device. The Soviet-made RPG-7 is a favorite weapon of the Iraqi insurgents.

Sadr Brigades Aka the Mehdi Army. Mullah Moktadar al-Sadr's Iranian-funded guerrilla army, which fought a series of unsuccessful campaigns against U.S. and Coalition forces in 2003, despite early victories over local Iraqi Police and National Guard forces.

SAW Squad Automatic Weapon. In the case of the U.S. Army troops in Iraq, a light .226-caliber machine gun, firing the same ammo as the M-16. Commonly mounted on Humvees, for convoy protection. Many soldiers prefer the heavier caliber .50-caliber machine gun, which matches up better with the Soviet-made 12.7-millimeter DshK. Similarly, many elite U.S. Army units prefer the AK-47 to the M-16 because of its heavier round.

Shi'a The faction of Islam founded by the Prophet Mohammed's descendants in opposition to the Sunnis, who chose a prominent early Moslem named Uthman as Caliph (leader of the faith). Shi'ism's leader, Hussein, was killed along with his family and followers by Sunni armies near the Iraqi city of Karbala in 680, and the Sunnis became the dominant sect. From early on, the Shi'a faith has been associated with the poor and disenfranchised, and its theology is permeated with ideas of political justice, egalitarianism and populism, while Sunnism, at least in the eyes of Shi'as, is the faith of the wealthy and powerful, kings and emperors. Shi'as, who constitute about 20 percent of all

Moslems worldwide, are a majority of the population in Lebanon, Iraq, and Iran, but everywhere except Iran they have been deprived of political power and suppressed. With the overthrow of Saddam Hussein's regime, Iraqi Shi'as now hope to control the new democratically elected government, through the electoral process. This prospect horrifies not only Iraqi Sunnis, who benefited greatly under the rule of their fellow-Sunni Saddam, but also the Shi'a mullahs who currently rule Iran; they fear that their subjects will begin looking to Iraqi Shi'a leaders like Ali al-Sistani and Kazwini for leadership. As the birthplace of Shi'ism, Iraq is the natural center of the faith; the Shi'a shrines and schools in Karbala, Hillah, and Najaf are far more famous than any in Iran, and the Iraqi Shi'a leaders are regarded as much more honest and unworldly.

"SIX" Military radio lingo for a unit's CO, or commanding officer. Used as a suffix: the soldiers of CAT-A 13, for instance, called themselves the Rogues, so Maj. Mark Clark was identified as "Rogue Six" on the radio. In larger units like battalions or companies, "Six" refers to the command element as a whole; the CO himself is referred to as "Six Actual."

TOC (Tactical Operations Center), the headquarters of a battalion in the field: It includes logistics, personnel, payroll, intelligence, transport and other vital command elements. The 425th CA Battalion's TOC was located near the main terminal at Baghdad International Airport, while elements of the 425th were scattered across BIAP, Camp Victory, the Baghdad area and as far south as the Shi'a city of Najaf.

USACAPOC (A) The U.S. Army Civil Affairs and Psychological Operations Command (Airborne), based at Fort Bragg, in Fayetteville, North Carolina. 97 percent of the five thousand troops under USACAPOC command are reservists, members of some two dozen CA and Psychological Operations battalions from all over the United States. There is only one full-time regular Army CA battalion, the 96th, also based at Bragg.

WAHABIS The puritanical reformist sect of Sunni Islam, founded in Saudi Arabia in the eighteenth century, that forms the theological basis for groups like the Taliban and al-Qaeda. Followers of a strict, humorless interpretation of the Koran, Wahabis are opposed to art, literature, mysticism, and all the great scholarly extrapolations from the Prophet's words that have taken place since Islam's founding. Because of their longtime alliance with the Saudi Arabian royal family, they wield much more power in the Islamic world than their small numbers warrant. Wahabis not only hate Christians and Jews, they regard non-Wahabi Moslems, including Shi'as, Sufis and moderate Sunnis, as *kaffirs* (unbelievers). In Iraq they have carried out attacks on both U.S. troops and the country's Shi'a majority.

AUTHOR'S NOTE

Some names and descriptions of individuals have been altered
to protect their privacy.

I was usually armed when I went out on Civil Affairs missions in Iraq, either with a borrowed M-16 or a 9mm Beretta
handgun I bought for $100 in the Baghdad black market. Al-
though I was a civilian—my ID card read PRESS, the tags on my
shirt said USACAPOC and CONTRACTOR, and the soldiers around
me knew me as "that crazy guy who's writing a book on Civil Affairs," aka "Writer Rob"—the units I was with in Baghdad were
so small that to burden them with a noncombatant guest would
have been unconscionable. I was another pair of eyes, another
finger on the trigger. As long as I was with the team, I was fully
prepared to fight in defense of them. It is important to empha-
size "defense": CA units never initiate combat; their mission is to
do aid and reconstruction work, and they fight only if they are
attacked in the course of their aid work and there is no alterna-
tive. In my opinion, there is nothing uglier than a reporter trying
to play Papa Hemingway, swaggering around with a shooting
iron, longing to put a notch on it.

PROLOGUE

Baghdad today, April 3, 2004, is the most wretched city on earth: dystopia with palm trees, a slice of hell beneath black smoke skies. The air is full of anxiety, malice and despair, spiking without warning into homicidal rage. The British writer Robert Byron visited here in 1933, and in his classic book *Road to Oxiana* he described the country in a classic passage: "a mud plain, so flat that a single heron, reposing on one leg beside some rare trickle of water in a ditch, looks as tall as a wireless aerial. From this plain rise villages of mud and cities of mud. The rivers flow with liquid mud. The air is composed of mud refined into a gas. Baghdad is the capital one would expect of this divinely favored land. It lurks in a mud fog; when the temperature drops below 110, the residents complain of the chill and get out their furs. For only one thing it is now justly famous: a kind of boil which takes nine months to heal, and leaves a scar."

You could quarrel with the particulars of Byron's description—dust instead of mud, a smoky, hazy, parboiled sky instead of a mud fog, and shabby, drab concrete and cinderblock buildings in place of mud hooches—but he definitely caught the grim essence of the place. Even his description of the fearsome boils: it may sound like something out of a medieval horror story, but it is all too true. The Department of Defense has warned all Iraq-bound personnel of the danger of sand-flea bites infected with something called leishamaniasis. The resultant lesions can produce leprosy-like tissue damage, eating away entire noses and ears. Many of us here are suffering from low-grade versions of the infection: bites that refuse to heal, that months later still keep you awake with itching and bleed without warning.

Today, in the aftermath of war, looting and economic collapse, the scene is particularly depressing. Baghdad's factories and public buildings are bombed-out hills of rubble or gutted, charred shells. Take a close look at that garbage dump: refugees have built shantytowns out of the toxic garbage, on the shores of poison-water lagoons. IEDs are everywhere, constructed from 155-millimeter rockets, RPG rounds and mortar shells; they are concealed inside concrete blocks, refuse heaps, black plastic bags and even dead road-killed animals, and placed along busy roads under cover of night. When the right target comes along, they are detonated by remote control, either cell phones or garage door openers.

A few days ago suicide bombers attacked Shi'a pilgrims at the al-Khadimiyah Shrine down the road, killing and maiming hundreds. Across the river, U.S. soldiers are locked in an endless war in the wretched slums of Sadr City; at night, fixed-wing gunships armed with Gatling guns and howitzers blast recalcitrant neighborhoods, but the violence inevitably flares up again. Haifa Street, the main thoroughfare through northwest Baghdad, has been off-limits to Coalition forces for months, Condition Red: it is hard-core bandit country, and if you go there, be ready to fight. (Imagine the Viet Cong camped out along K Street in Washington, D.C.: you get the idea.)

Even the big U.S. bases like Baghdad International Airport, Camp Victory and the Green Zone are not safe. They get hit by rockets and mortar fire on a regular basis. Planes taking off and landing at BIAP perform wild evasive maneuvers, corkscrewing and juking to avoid gunfire and surface-to-air missiles. Every week U.S. soldiers and civilians are killed in ambushes and by IEDs and suicide car bombers on Route Irish, the main highway from the airport to the Green Zone downtown.

In the midst of all this, at seven-thirty in the morning, CAT-A 13 of the 425th Civil Affairs Battalion is preparing to go out and do good deeds. Seven soldiers, Army reservists, in two unarmored open-backed Humvees, off to win hearts and minds.

Officially, the team's AO is the al-Khadimiyah neighborhood in northwestern Baghdad, but CAT-A 13's CO Maj. Mark Clark believes in thinking and acting in ways his superiors characterize as "outside the box," helping Iraqis no matter where they are, even if their problems aren't covered in the battalion's official orders. Today's missions are way across the Tigris, in the heart of eastern Baghdad, and they are not really part of CAT-A 13's official responsibilities.

First of all, the Major has a legal document he needs to deliver. Several months ago, before the Major and the rest of his battalion arrived in-country, an Iraqi soldier got caught in a long gasoline queue at a service station in al-Khadimiyah. He attempted to jump the line, and when a couple of local security guards tried to stop him he began waving his AK-47 around, threatening to fire up the crowd of waiting motorists. An American patrol arrived on the scene, and in the ensuing scuffle one of the GIs shot and wounded the crazed Iraqi soldier. The GI signed an affidavit taking responsibility for the shooting, and all the Iraqi witnesses agreed that it was completely justified, but somehow the security guards ended up being arrested and jailed for the incident. They are currently out on bail, but as things stand now they may well end up back behind bars; the Iraqi justice system is notoriously corrupt and unjust. Major Clark has taken it upon himself to try and exonerate the two men; he has a copy of the affidavit, which he hopes will persuade an east Baghdad appeals judge to drop the charges.

The second mission is to give toys to orphans. One of Major Clark's many Iraqi contacts has told him about a new orphanage that is opening up today in east Baghdad, near the courthouse. Friends of the team members back in the States have sent over several cartons of brand-new toys, and the team is going to the opening ceremony to hand them out.

The members of CAT-A 13 gather in the driveway of the team house compound, and Sgt. Bob Paul, a sharp-tongued former Peace Corps volunteer, runs through the convoy briefing. "Everyone got a full combat load of ammo? Radios working? Water and MREs? Snivel gear?" This last refers to toilet paper, sunscreen and any other comfort items a soldier might want to bring along. I pat my pants pocket, making sure I have my daily can of chewing tobacco, and I notice Sergeant Grundman doing the same as he climbs up into the back of the lead Humvee. Snuff is the perfect drug for war zones: it kills the time between crises, and delivers a subtle combination of anesthesia and sensory kick. Brigade quartermaster, the giant mail order military gear supplier, has begun marketing a holsterlike watertight and airtight snuff holder that fits on a military web belt, for field-expedient dipping.

"Remember, if we're threatened, always use the graduated response—*shout, shove, show and shoot,*" Sergeant Paul continues. "If someone makes a threatening move, first shout at him. If that doesn't work, shove him. If he keeps on coming, show your weapon, and point it at him. If he doesn't stop then, go ahead and shoot him, and aim to kill—aim for the main body mass."

"And don't shoot all over the place and hit a bunch of innocent bystanders," Major Clark interjects. "We didn't come here to get ourselves killed, but one dead kid or little old lady and we've undone everything good we're trying to do."

"Aw, I want to shoot a little old lady," Spec. Shane Cruddas mock-complains; he is a hulking young Hispanic kid from the wrong side of the tracks in L.A., who just turned twenty-one yesterday.

"If a bunch of ragheads come after us, I'm shooting every motherfucking one of them," the team's official redneck and gnarly ex-Marine sniper, Sergeant Kramer, says, with a carnivorous crocodile grin.

"No, you're not," Major Clark says to both of them, smiling. I've only been with CAT-A 13 two or three days, but I've already learned that this kind of joking around is typical. When they are out in the field, the team is all business, as serious as a heart attack, but between missions they are loose and informal. It's their style.

"Be on the lookout for Iraqis and foreigners in civilian clothing," Sergeant Paul continues. "They may be in small groups, armed with automatic weapons and RPGs. Watch for people with video cameras—we've got reports the Bad Guys are videotaping our convoys, to learn how we operate, so they can attack us more easily. Also watch for Bad Guys in Iraqi police uniforms. Intel says they may be setting up fake checkpoints, to try and stop Coalition convoys and shoot them up. If you see a checkpoint and it doesn't look right, speed up and drive through it. If they shoot at us, shoot back. We can always apologize later, but not if we're dead. That's it."

He turns to Major Clark. "Anything to add, sir?"

"Nope. Let's go."

Cruddas takes the wheel of the lead Humvee: a perfect choice for driver, as his favorite leisure activity back home is customizing and street-racing hot rods. Major Clark sits next to him, and Grundman is in the rear, alongside Kramer, who is manning the SAW-gun. Sgt. Lynn Goff, a short, wide Sacramento farm girl, is driving the number two Hummer, with Sergeant Paul next to her. Sergeant Lawrence, inexplicably known as "Fat Larry" (if anything, he is underweight), is in the backseat, while surfer girl Jen Espinoza, aka Espi, is in the rear, on the tail SAW. I am back there with her.

All the team members are wearing Kevlar helmets, and body armor with front and rear trauma plates designed to stop an AK-47 round: bulky stuff, that weighs a good twenty-five pounds. Over the back of the armored vest is a camelback hydration system, a rubber bladder containing at least half a gallon of water: you can drink from its flexible plastic tube whenever you are thirsty, no matter what you are doing. Army regulations also mandate ballistic goggles, to protect against shrapnel, debris and dust. I am decked out in the same gear as the soldiers. We look like semihuman, sumoesque characters from a hybrid sci-fi film, *Star Wars Meets Dune.*

We leave the team compound and head out through Banzai FOB, the fortified post that is home to the 1/5 Cav Battalion and CAT-A 13. Just before the main gate we stop one last time for the team members to load their M-16s, handguns and SAWs. I shove a clip into the Beretta and make sure the safety is on. The guards open the gate, and we pull out into the lethal reality of Baghdad.

We drive south along the Tigris, and then pull up onto the bridge to east Baghdad. Across the river a pair of attack choppers cruises, keeping a wary eye on Sadr City; the other night an RPG nearly took out a low-flying U.S. gunship. A couple of flat-bottomed native boats drift downriver, fishing for carp or smuggling weapons, who knows? The insurgents have been using boats to ferry guns and explosives from east Baghdad to al-Khadimiyah, avoiding potential checkpoints on the bridges; the arms are stashed somewhere in the neighborhood, ready for some future Tet Offensive, Night of the Long Knives. Far to the southwest a column of black oily smoke unravels skyward, the aftermath of an IED or a car bomb explosion, probably on Route Irish or near the Green Zone. A gust from the hot north wind carries the sound of a heavy machine gun, a burst of harsh bangs like someone beating on an empty oil drum with a crowbar. "Just another day in Paradise," as the soldiers like to say.

As we enter east Baghdad, everyone goes on hyper-alert. No one on CAT-A 13 has been here before, and new places are always dangerous in a war zone. Eyes peer down side streets, into the dark cavernous interiors of bombed-out buildings, scan rooftops, watching for the flicker of a machine-gun muzzle flash, the puff of dust of an RPG being fired, a furtive pedestrian or someone who doesn't look right, ducking or moving too fast. Survival in Iraq is literally a matter of split seconds. A moment's carelessness can mean a lifetime of pain and regret, dead friends, lost limbs or simply life cut short, *finis, nada.*

We weave our way through the heavy traffic, cars, vans, minibuses, buses, trucks, an occasional horse cart or an old man or a boy riding a donkey. There are surprising numbers of expensive cars, models none of the CAT-A 13 soldiers could ever afford back home: Opel town cars, Mercedes-Benzes, high-end Japanese sedans. Many of the Bad Guys who attack U.S. convoys seem to drive luxury rides. When we pass a big black Benz with smoked windows and four scowling youths inside, Major Clark radios from the lead Humvee: "Keep an eye on that Mercedes."

Espi does more than that: she swings the SAW-gun over and points it right at the driver, who brakes hard and swerves off onto a side street. I don't blame her. Almost every day you convoy through Baghdad, somebody tries something, pulls a feint or sees what they can get away with. Better safe than sorry.

After about half an hour it becomes obvious we are lost. We don't have GPS cooordinates for either the courthouse or the orphanage, just written directions, and these, it turns out, are murky at best. Every few minutes we stop and the Major and Espi dismount and ask directions in their halting Arabic. Major Clark is studying Conversational Iraqi Arabic from a bunch of books he has brought with him, and Espi is a natural at languages: she was near the top of her class in Mandarin Chinese at the Army Language School in Monterey when the Army ganked her for duty in Iraq. So far the locals seem friendly; one little boy even insists on running along next to our two vehicles till he is sure we have found the right intersection. At last we find the courthouse. Major Clark grabs the legal papers and goes inside, only to exit two minutes later. This is the wrong courthouse: you have to go to a different one for felony appeals, though nobody inside is sure which. "Well, we'll just have to try again another day," the Major says.

We continue on, looking for the orphanage, but that doesn't pan out either. Iraqis on the street say, "Yes, there is an orphanage over here somewhere, it actually opened a few days ago," but they don't know where it is. The Major and Sergeant Paul confer, and decide to return to al-Khadimiyah and resume the team's missions there.

We are heading back toward the Tigris when the day begins to go south in spades. We keep losing our way in the unfamiliar mazeways of west Baghdad. Finally we find a major thoroughfare, a wide four-lane avenue that seems to lead in the right direction, and we turn onto it. We have gone a half-dozen blocks when we notice something about the people on the sidewalk: there seem to be more and more of them, and they look like they have a common purpose. The traffic begins to slow down ahead, and then back up. About the same time we grind to a halt, the pedestrian masses coalesce into a crowd, a mob. There are big black and green banners here and there. Someone is yelling into a bullhorn, and people are shouting and chanting. Individuals in the crowd point at us and give us angry looks. The traffic is gridlocked in front, behind and on all sides. We have inadvertently driven into a huge anti-American demonstration, and we can't get out of it.

I suddenly realize that we haven't seen any other American troops, not a single vehicle or check post, since we crossed the river. We are alone and completely on our own; from overlords to underdogs in a few wrong turns. This is the archetypal nightmare of the East, to be caught in a sea, a whirlpool of hostile natives, that could swallow you up in an instant and not leave a trace: shades of *Zulu,* Custer's Last Stand, Gordon at Khartoum.

Just ahead the street splits, the right lane spooling off around the traffic circle, the left lane descending into a tunnel that comes out on the far side of the roundabout. The right lane isn't really an option: it leads right into the roiling center mass of the crowd.

After a brief consultation over the radio, Major Clark and Sergeant Paul concur, and when the traffic moves forward again we head down into the underpass. A few car lengths short of the mouth of the tunnel we find ourselves stalled again, as the traffic comes to a complete halt. We are eye to eye with the scores of demonstrators who are perched along the top of the underpass. Now we are trapped underground, and more and more of the Iraqis are gathering to watch us.

Espi turns to me: "Hey, Rob, if someone throws a grenade in here, kick it out, okay?" Her tone is casual, like she is asking me to hand her a can of soda. I tell her no worries, I've got her back. I have my handgun out, holding it out of sight of the demonstrators, below the side of the Humvee. Everyone on the team is watching a different part of the crowd and the surrounding cars, 360-degree awareness; at the same time, they all manage to look totally relaxed, like this is exactly where they are supposed to be, everything is AOK, no problem. No weapons are raised, no one is shouting, no one is yelling on the radio or pointing frantically here and there; CAT-A 13 is an eye of calm in the maelstrom.

This is unmistakably Major Clark's team, and it has drawn its character from him. Clark is ex–Special Forces; like the Navy SEALs and Delta Force operators, Special Forces soldiers are hardcore gunslingers, expert combat troops, but they differ from the other elite U.S. units in one very important respect: they are trained to work with indigenous peoples, to win them over, train them and lead them against a common enemy. You are not a good SF soldier unless you can fit in anywhere you are sent. In places like occupied Iraq it is a soldierly skill at least as valuable as map-reading or marksmanship, and it shows through now.

Sergeant Paul gets out to check out the traffic up ahead, and he immediately draws the attention of a group of street kids leaning on the railing above. They start yelling at him, and instead of pretending not to hear them or raising his gun and the stakes, he yells back: not angrily, it is more like he and the kids are trading wisecracks. One of the kids comes back at Sarge with something that makes him bust out laughing despite himself. The sight of a gun-toting American soldier laughing at himself provokes the little hoodlums into ecstasy: they are high-fiving and cheering each other.

Meanwhile Kramer gets on the radio to our Humvee and says, "Hey, tell Espi and Writer Rob if the motherfuckers start closing in they can always throw the goddamn toys at them." That gets every team member within earshot laughing as well. There are puzzled, quizzical looks on the faces of many of the Iraqis watching; they must be wondering why these soldiers seem so calm and relaxed, unthreatened and unthreatening.

Major Clark gets out of the front Humvee, and he saunters in his great cowpoke stride up to the front of the vehicle and surveys the scene, his M-16 dangling carelessly from one hand. The Major is a fanatical John Wayne fan; he even *looks* like a cross between an old-fashioned silver-screen sheriff and a Great Plains Indian chief, with his lanky frame and hawk-eyed hatchet face. When he catches a couple of motorists staring at him, he grins disarmingly back at them and waves. The Iraqis hesitate, then wave back.

Sergeant Paul intercepts him, and I hear him asking if we shouldn't just smash through the fence into the other lane and weave our way out through the opposing traffic beneath the tunnel. The Rules of Engagement allow us to drive on the sidewalks, jump medians and crash through people's yards to get out of trouble. Major Clark shakes his head: "I'd rather not do that. It sets a bad example for the Iraqis." Sergeant Paul nods, shrugs, smiles.

Walking up a couple of car lengths, Major Clark sees there are gaps in the stalled traffic; also, the fence between the two lanes ends after about fifty feet. He starts going from car to car, talking to the drivers, smiling, gesturing. As the vehicles begin to move up at his direction, he calls to Cruddas to get ready to move.

Space opens up in front of us. As both Humvees start to roll, the Major and Sergeant Paul jump aboard. We accelerate past the fence, bounce up over the low concrete median and head the wrong way through the tunnel; there is just enough room for us to squeeze through the oncoming traffic with inches to spare. Always the Hearts and Minds Brigade, the soldiers smile and make apologetic gestures at the Iraqi drivers, who look more bemused and amused than outraged at the crazy infidels driving on the wrong side of the road. As we emerge on the far side of the circle, we jump back over the median and take the first street in the direction of the Tigris. Looking back, I can see more trucks of black-uniformed youths with green armbands arriving, and more people on foot streaming into the plaza. The scene is rapidly approaching critical mass, like a gigantic red-hot frying pan full of corn beginning to pop.

The street is almost empty for the next couple of blocks, and then we come to another crowd, gathered in front of a big mosque. Loudspeakers are thundering the mullah's sermon from inside. The mood here seems different: there are no banners or uniforms, and people are so intent on the mullah's words they barely notice us.

As we pass by, an ancient woman swaddled in black emerges from the mosque, sees us and starts running toward us across the sidewalk, beating her breast with her fists. Tears are streaming down her face, which is so deeply wrinkled and furrowed it looks like a geological specimen. When she reaches the edge of the sidewalk, she falls to her knees and cries out to us: "*Thank you! Thank you, Ameriki!*" Nobody knows what to think, or what to do. As we drive past her, we wave and smile, even hardhearted kill-'em-all Kramer: I see his mouth form the word "Thanks." And then there is the bridge across the Tigris we have been looking for. We accelerate, and Irene it across to the friendlier shores of west Baghdad, and home.

Afterward, I ask Sergeant Paul about his dialogue with the street kid, the one that left the urchins laughing and helped defuse the situation. He immediately laughs: "I thought I'd be funny, so I yelled to him in English, 'Why don't you kiss my balls?' He was really pissing me off, and it was a way of letting off steam. And then the kid yelled back to me in perfect English, 'Only if you show them to me first.' Smart little bastard—all I could do was laugh. He really nuked me."

The orphanage we were seeking remains a mystery. According to Iraqis we ask, it's on the west side of the Tigris instead of the east, or it hasn't opened yet, or maybe it doesn't exist at all. The boxes of toys go back into the team house storage room. They end up being distributed to various schools and orphanages, and at the daylong walk-in medical clinics the team later runs with doctors from the 1/5 Cav.

The mosque we drove by, with the old weeping woman, was one loyal to Imam Ali al-Sistani, the traditional leader of Iraqi's Shi'as who lives in the holy city of Najaf; he has been counseling his followers to be patient and cooperate with the Americans, as long as we deliver on our promises to rebuild the country and then leave. During the Saddam era he survived three or four assassination attempts by the Baghdad regime, and saw hundreds of thousands of his fellow Shi'as massacred in the aftermath of the Gulf War, when the first President Bush called on the Shi'as of Iraq to rise up against Saddam's government and then stood by and watched them die. He is a man of almost supernatural patience, and political savvy: he knows when all is said and done his people will inherit the country in which their religion was born and where they now compose two-thirds of the population. It's only a matter of time, and al-Sistani lives in a totally different time zone than we Americans do.

That mob we blundered into at the traffic circle, they're a totally different story. Although we didn't know it at the time, those black-uniformed thugs in the trucks were the Mehdi Army, or the Sadr Brigades, the soon-to-be-infamous guerrilla force organized by the militant young mullah Moktadar al-Sadr. We were the first U.S. troops to run into them. This same afternoon, after we have made it back to al-Khadimiyah, these same fighters and thousands more like them begin attacking U.S. convoys and posts throughout the Shi'a portion of Iraq. Over the next few weeks and months, Coalition troops and the Iraqi National Guard and police will fight a series of small wars with the Mehdi Army, from Baghdad to Najaf and Karbala to Basra in the far south.

Al-Sadr doesn't believe in waiting; he wants it all right now, America out and Iraq for the Iraqis, specifically him and *his* Iraqis: why should the people suffer under foreign invaders when they can suffer under their own homegrown religious dictatorship? Of course, the Mehdi Army isn't exactly homegrown: we would find out later it has been funded by the Iranians to the tune of several tens of millions of dollars. Over time his Iranian connection would prove to be a real problem for al-Sadr: most Iraqi Shi'as dislike Iran far more than they like their Iranian coreligionists, with ethnicity trumping faith, and al-Sadr never does attract a mass following. Most Iraqi Shi'as, especially in traditional neighborhoods like al-Khadimiyah, prefer the leadership of cagy old al-Sistani.

PART I

CIVIL AFFAIRS

1

I FIRST BECAME fascinated with the U.S. Army's Civil Affairs program during a trip to Afghanistan, back in the autumn of 2002.

I had first visited the country in 1984, more or less by accident; I was on my way from Europe to India, overland, to research my Ph.D. thesis in anthropology, and Afghanistan happened to be in the way. That first visit had led to others, more than twenty in all by now; most of them were during the Soviet invasion, when I worked as a correspondent, aid worker and war crimes investigator.

The trip before that, shortly after 9/11, I had watched B-52s bomb Taliban and al-Qaeda troops off a ridgeline above the resistance-held town of Khojabauhuddin. Children clutching school bags made from yellow plastic U.S.-aid food parcels cheered and hugged my knees. When I traveled east to the city of Faizabad, the locals were celebrating the Taliban defeat in classic Afghan fashion, filling the night with torrents of machine-gun tracer fire, rockets and artillery rounds. After years of seeing the country suffer under the Soviets and the homegrown and foreign fanatics who followed, it was pure joy.

After that trip, I had begun hearing about the U.S. Army's Civil Affairs program that was starting up in Afghanistan. There were thirteen small CA teams, called "Chiclets" (Coalition Humanitarian Liaison Cells), scattered across the country, working to help the Afghans rebuild. I decided I had to go back and see what kind of job they were doing. Over time I had learned to be cynical about America's role in Afghanistan. After the Soviet defeat, the U.S. government had repaid the Afghans' trust by turning the country over to the Pakistanis, their Taliban surrogates and the Taliban's Arab fundamentalist bankers: cheap oil from Saudi Arabia, and a potentially lucrative pipeline route across Afghanistan, outweighed honor. It was only when terrorists based in Afghanistan attacked the United States that we intervened and, almost as an afterthought, liberated the long-suffering Afghan people. I wanted to see just how genuine the U.S. Army's aid efforts were, so I decided to go back and see, and write an article about what I found for *Time* magazine.

The team I chose to visit in 2002 was stationed in the Bamiyan Valley, in the mountains of central Afghanistan. I had done aid work in Bamiyan three or four years before, helping the local Hazara tribespeople as they fought against the forces of the Taliban and their al-Qaeda allies. The valley was conquered by the Taliban after I left; they proceeded to virtually destroy everything there, and only stopped when the U.S. and its Afghan allies drove them out after 9/11. I figured that since I knew the area well, and since it was such a total disaster area, it would be a perfect place for me to take the measure of Civil Affairs.

I arrived in what was left of Bamiyan after a daylong drive from Kabul, north cross the Shomali Plains and then west, over high mountains and through narrow, crooked gorges. The last leg of the journey was through Hazara territory, and I began to see the destruction the Taliban had wrought there. Villages were burned out, abandoned, fields fallow; even the fruit trees and willow windbreaks had been chopped down. In one or two places, surviving families had returned home: men and women were threshing grain, and children were driving livestock in from the fields. These isolated islands of light and life in the cold autumn dusk made the overall desolation seem only more forlorn and heartbreaking. When I reached the town itself, the destruction was even worse, more dramatic. Bamiyan was the capital of the two million-odd members of the Hazara tribe, and before it fell to the Taliban it had been a thriving center of trade and government: Hizb-i-Wahdat, the Hazara tribal political party, published newspapers and literary and women's magazines; there were girls' schools in the local mosques and in caves and a multi-ethnic coeducational university in a compound near the eastern edge of town. The two biggest Buddha images in the world, carved out of the sandstone cliffs fifteen hundred years ago, watched over the valley like guardians.

Now all this was gone. Ninety percent of the buildings in town were demolished, blown up or burned. The once-thriving main bazaar was mostly rubble. The university compound lay in ruins; reportedly the Taliban had murdered hundreds of the students and stuffed their bodies down the well in the corner of the compound, and then turned the place into their headquarters.

As American and Afghan resistance forces approached the valley, the local Taliban troops rallied there and prepared to fight. Unknown to them, a spy satellite was watching. Less than an hour later, one of our planes dropped a thousand-pound smart bomb smack on the center of the building, interring the entire Taliban garrison beneath the rubble: murderers buried on top of their innocent victims. Even the valley's great Buddhas were gone, dynamited into dust by the fanatical Taliban, leaving eerie vacant niches in the cliffs.

In all of this desolation Chiclet-5, the U.S. Army Civil Affairs team in Bamiyan, was a revelation. It had just six members, five of them reservists from the Knoxville-based 489th CA Battalion: Lt. Col. Roger Walker and four young sergeants. The sixth man was a regular Army communications specialist from the Pacific Northwest, who had volunteered for the mission. Like most CA teams they were basically on their own, with only a couple of other small Army units close enough to call on for help, and the nearest big U.S. base, at Bagram, several hours away across the mountains.

During the winter Shebar Pass, the sole way in and out of the eastern end of the valley, was blocked by snow for weeks at a time; supplies, when they came at all, were airdropped in. In today's world of high-tech weaponry and computer-generated battlefield scenarios, it was like stepping back in time to the era of *Lawrence of Arabia* or *The Man Who Would Be King*.

They were underfunded, overworked, and they had to keep a constant eye out for snipers, mines and ambushes: the Taliban had put a $5,000 bounty per man on their heads. But they were still outperforming all of the U.N. agencies, NGOs, and aid programs in the valley put together. All you had to do was ask the locals; almost everyone I talked to expressed scorn for the overpaid, overbureaucratic civilian aid workers and praised the job the Chiclets were doing.

The Chiclet team's post was a scorpion-infested abandoned stone hotel on a cliff overlooking the town. It was an austere place, with bare concrete floors and venomous camel spiders the size of saucers lurking in the walls. There was a communal outhouse down the hill; barnlike outbuildings housed vehicles, workshops and the guard room for the Hazara militia troops who helped with security. The whole thing was surrounded by barbed wire seeded with antipersonnel mines and trip flares.

The place had a jerry-rigged, improvised air, kind of like Chiclet-5 itself. None of the six team members, Lt. Col. Roger Walker and his four sergeants or the regular Army soldier, Spec. Germaine Watson, had ever met before the mission. When 9/11 came down, they had immediately been called up and thrown into the breach. The team's first meeting was on the plane flying over from Germany into Kabul.

They had a funny style, these six soldiers: they behaved more like a family of rowdy brothers, or best friends, than an elite military unit. When I asked Sergeant Groce what he thought of Colonel Walker, he made sure his CO was within earshot, and then said loudly, "He throws things at us, and beats us with broomsticks. But I still love him, and I'm not ashamed to say it!" Groce pretended to weep with emotion, and turned to Walker. "You love me, too, don't you, sir?" he implored.

"Oh, yeah," Colonel Walker said sarcastically, with a wide grin. "I don't even want to go home anymore, I just want to stay here with you."

The team members had given each other comical, highly abusive and inevitably obscene radio call signs: Colonel Walker was "Snatch," McElhay was "Manwhore," and other noms de guerre included "Mangina" and the comparatively benign "Sonic Hedgehog." A neat computer-printed sign someone planted on McElhay's door read, MANWHORE LOVES IT.

And what kind of job was this seemingly motley crew doing?
If I hadn't seen it for myself, I never would have believed it. In
just one of their two dozen or so ongoing aid projects, the Chiclets had rebuilt a village school destroyed by the Taliban, only
to find that the impoverished villagers had no school supplies,
not even a single pencil, and there was no money for educational
materials in the Army's budget for the project. Colonel Walker
e-mailed his relatives back home, explaining the problem and
asking for help. An elderly aunt in Texas organized a bake sale at
her church, raised more than a thousand dollars, bought three
hundred pounds of everything from teachers' kits to notebooks,
pens and art supplies, and mailed them via the APO to Bamiyan!
One glorious night a C-130 made its supply drop, and among the
boxes that fell from the sky were the precious tools for learning.

Aided by a few Special Forces troops temporarily stationed
in the area along with local militia members, the CA team trucked
the cargo up to the new schoolhouse. One of the regular Army
soldiers helping out was a young woman from upstate New York,
Spec. Alison Kastner. Her eyes teared as a horde of raggedy children with hopeful, expectant faces poured from the school.

"I'd just like to hold every single one of them," she said.

"So would I," Colonel Walker replied in a gruff, husky voice.

It was like a scene from an old-fashioned corny movie, only
better: it was real.

Then there was the tent encampment of landless refugee
families stranded on a barren mesa north of town. They had
been living in the old Buddhist monks' caves below the site of
the big Buddhas, but the local Afghans didn't want them
around: Bamiyan had enough troubles of its own without taking
on those of outsiders. A certain French NGO bowed to political

pressure and trucked the two hundred or so men, women and children to the mesa, put them in worn-out canvas tents and left them there with no food, water, medical care, anything: basically left them to die. Colonel Walker had a succinct comment about the guilty aid workers: "They really shit in their own hats."

The colonel, with a rural American's root instinct for fair play, had virtually adopted the refugees. The team brought them food and water, hired as many of the men as possible as laborers on their school and bridge-building projects and lobbied the Bamiyan officials to either let the refugees move back into the caves or allow them to move into some of the town's many abandoned dwellings for the winter. By December, blizzards would be dumping waist-deep snow and sending temperatures to minus-thirty: there was no way the refugees would survive till spring in those flimsy tents.

When the local powers that be still refused to help the refugees, the indefatigable Colonel Walker set up a new aid project, hiring blacksmiths to make stoves out of the abundant military scrap metal, selling half the stoves to pay the smiths and giving the rest to the refugees to heat their tents. Meanwhile he wrote to the Hazara tribe's chief, Qadir Khalili, in Kabul, asking him to intervene and order his people in Bamiyan to let the refugees move back into the caves. Khalili and the colonel were great friends, and Colonel Walker was confident the chief would come to the refugees' rescue before the first snows fell.

When we visited the refugees' camp, Colonel Walker and his Chiclets were greeted with something close to adulation. Women held up their newborn babies for the colonel to admire, children gazed at him with awestruck eyes, and the men addressed him as "Colonel-*jan*"—"Dear Colonel."

* * *

Two days before I arrived in Bamiyan, the team had gotten orders to start wearing regulation Army uniforms in the field. Previously the CA troops in Afghanistan had worn the same loose pajama-like pants and shirts as the local Afghans. It was a matter of security, as Colonel Walker explained: "Some Bad Guy sees us driving by, and it takes him an extra few seconds to ID us as Americans, and by then we're gone. Now it's, 'Hey, look!—' Bang, bang, bang, you're dead."

Rumors are as numerous as beans and bullets in the Army, and the unpopular and inexplicable uniform change gives birth to at least two. Interestingly they both cast blame outside the Special Forces/Special Operations community, on either a non-SF/SO Pentagon desk jockey or, worse, a civilian meddler. According to one story, some big-bottomed golf-playing general back in the States had seen a magazine photo of Special Forces troops in beards and tribal clothes patrolling the Khyber Pass with their Afghan auxiliaries, blew his stack and ordered all the SF and CA troops in Afghanistan to shave and don "proper" uniforms.

Another story I heard from some Special Forces troops blamed the order on a bigwig from a private aid group who dropped in on an SF team up on the Khyber Pass; when he wasn't treated with sufficient "respect" by the SFers, he swore he was going to go back to Washington and use his "important friends" there to put an end to what he called the "undisciplined lifestyle" of the Special Forces soldiers. The fact that this order might eventually kill American soldiers evidently never occurred to the gold-stars-and-braid brigade back home on the Potomac.

Of course, Special Forces has its own friendly powers in the nation's capital; a few phone calls, and they were back in their *shalwar kameezes* again and sporting beards, just like the Hindu Kush hillbillies they worked among. Civil Affairs troops, lacking the SFers' clout, were stuck with the b.s. order. The Bamiyan Chiclets had obeyed the command, but they didn't like it. To Colonel Walker, it was eerily reminiscent of the British redcoats in the American Revolution, marching to battle in starched uniforms that were like giant "Shoot Me" signs. "At least I'll look Strac* when they body-bag me," one of the sergeants said with a grim smile.

At the same time, the Chiclets were dead serious about their role as combat soldiers. They observed strict security on the road, with two Americans and at least two Afghans holding weapons at the ready at all times. Before they left the post, Colonel Walker always ran through the drill for land mines: "If your vehicle hits a mine, everyone who's alive and conscious give a thumbs-up so the rest can see who's down and who's okay. If you take fire, un-ass the vehicle on the opposite side and roll to the nearest ditch. If you've got a weapon, lay down suppressive fire. Someone will be on the radio calling in backup—we can have Blackhawks and A-10s here in twenty minutes from Bagram."

When the colonel visited the bazaar to meet with his subcontractors, Sergeants Groce and McElhay sprinted to opposite ends of the street, McElhay with his M-16, Groce humping the big M-60, while Spec. Germaine Watson monitored the radio. At night, team members pulled guard duty from sunset to sunup

---

*****Strac** Longtime Army slang for dress and behavior that follow military regulations so slavishly they are downright obnoxious and/or risible.

in four shifts, scanning the perimeter of the post through a third-generation Starlite scope from the hotel's sandbagged roof. A couple of times each week the team members honed their shooting skills in a ravine above the airstrip, firing M-16s, M-60s and 9mm pistols. Their favorite targets were the big cans of shaving cream the Army inexplicably included in every sundry kit the men received—"Enough shaving cream every month to float an aircraft carrier," someone commented. When you hit them square, they exploded in a spectacular geyser of foam. "I hope Taliban and al-Qaeda come after us," Colonel Walker said matter-of-factly, not boasting, just quietly telling it like it is. If it's true it ain't bragging, as they say in the South. "And if they do they'd better come loaded for bear, because we're good, real good."

Like all too many Americans, I had thought heroes were a thing of the past; or, if they existed, the realities of the modern world rendered their deeds meaningless. After all, what could one man or woman, or even a handful, do that would make a positive impact, when matched up against the problems of billions of people, weapons of mass destruction, mega-famines and plagues, and wars that never seemed to end? The age of courage and right action seemed to be gone, if it had ever existed at all.

Meeting Colonel Walker and his men, seeing what they accomplished, was a true revelation, like a lightning flash out of nowhere in the darkness. They were risking their lives every day in order to build a future for a forgotten people betrayed by the rest of the world. They were everyday Americans, regular Joes, your next-door neighbors and mine, but through true grit and sheer nerve they had become heroes, the stuff of myths and legends.

2

WHEN I RETURNED to the States and began to try and find out more about Civil Affairs, I immediately discovered that it wasn't easy. Very little has been written on the subject; the only real "Civil Affairs book" is John Hersey's novel *A Bell for Adano*, and that is about a CA officer working in a Sicilian fishing village in the aftermath of World War Two: great stuff, but it is fiction, and half a century old at that. Most Americans today are barely aware of Civil Affairs. It is the U.S. military's great untold story.

Second, I found that CA is a uniquely American invention that goes far back in our history and has played an important ongoing role in shaping our nation's destiny. American soldiers began doing Civil Affairs–type work more than one hundred and fifty years ago, during the Mexican-American War, and our armies have continued helping defeated enemies recover and occupied countries improve themselves ever since then.

The godfather of CA, Gen. Winfield Scott, was a gentle bear of a man, who in his prime stood six foot three and weighed over 250 pounds. Scott was at once a career soldier, a brilliant military tactician and a hard-core unapologetic humanitarian. He first distinguished himself during President Andrew Jackson's infamous removal of the Cherokee Indians from their ancestral lands in Georgia and the Carolinas and their forced march along the "Trail of Tears" to Oklahoma. Placed in charge of the mass eviction, Scott insisted on allowing the Cherokees themselves to organize and lead their migration west, saving hundreds of Indian lives in the process. Jackson, along with the rabble-rousing newspapers of the day, castigated Scott as an "Indian lover," but the big general went ahead and carried out his mission his way.

When war broke out with Mexico in 1846, Scott led the American expeditionary force in a deft, skillful campaign that quickly achieved victory while avoiding massive casualties on both sides. It was after the Mexican surrender that the general issued the radical set of commands that mark the beginning of Civil Affairs in the U.S. military. In an era when newspapers routinely referred to Hispanics as "greasers," and Anglo frontiersmen could kill Mexicans with impunity, and frequently did, he ordered his troops to treat the native inhabitants with respect, and he set them to work building schools and roads in the countryside. When the American forces prepared to go home in 1848, a delegation of locals came to Scott's headquarters and begged the general to stay on as president of their country.

Over the next century, the U.S. military would follow Scott's enlightened precedent in war zones around the world, from Haiti to the Philippines. It was as if there were two sides to the American heart, one violent, even brutal, the other generous and compassionate, and they were both on display everywhere our Manifest Destiny took us.

During that age of unabashed interventionism, the Marine Corps was the point of America's imperial sword, and through trial, error and a lot of Yankee ingenuity the Leathernecks became experts in nation-building, repairing and renovating. The Marine Small Wars Handbook, first published in 1940, is a compendium of that expertise, and it is as hip and germane today as it was when the lessons learned were first jotted down a hundred years ago.

"The motive in small wars is not material destruction," the manual states. Instead, it is the opposite: "the social, economic, and political development of the people." To accomplish this, occupation troops should treat the local population with "tolerance, sympathy and kindness." A successful occupation requires that "all ranks be familiar with . . . the language, the geography, and the political, social and economic" conditions in the occupied country. Troops are particularly warned to avoid any actions showing "criticism or lack of respect for the religious beliefs and practices observed by the native inhabitants. . . . The more one shows a fraternal spirit, the easier will be the task," the manual goes on to say, and it stresses how bonding between occupation forces and occupied peoples depends on the ability to communicate: "If not already familiar with the language [of the occupied country], all officers upon assignment to expeditionary duty should study and acquire a working knowledge of it,"

For years, when the manual was out of print, CA officers haunted used-book stores and spent a hundred dollars or more for a dog-eared copy; recently it has been reissued in paperback, and many Civil Affairs COs and team leaders carry copies with them in the field now.

The aftermath of World War Two would mark the high tide of CA. During the war years there had been a spirited debate within the Roosevelt administration over who should be in charge of pacifying and rehabilitating our defeated foes, the military or the civilian arm of the government. In the end the generals prevailed, and it fell to the U.S. Army, employing thousands of highly trained aid workers and administrators, to rebuild Occupied Germany and Japan from the rubble up, instituting democratic systems and prosperous free market economies that still endure to this day.

While researching Civil Affairs, I had the chance to talk with one of these benign old warriors. The son of German-Jewish immigrants in New York, Herman Frankel enlisted in the infantry in 1943; the Army took note of his intelligence and education, and sent him back to college to study German. As the war in Europe ended, he was sent to Bavaria, where he helped de-Nazify the local government and assisted the Germans in rebuilding their devastated towns and cities.

"Some of the local people had ideas for opening small factories and workshops," Frankel recalls, "but there was no place to put them. Every major building had been bombed out, destroyed. The only suitable place turned out to be an old concentration camp. I helped them fix the buildings up, and they moved in there and started hiring workers and manufacturing goods."

By the time Frankel left the Army (he was Colonel Frankel by then), he had many close German friends, decent people who had never succumbed to Nazism back during the Hitler era and who appreciated this American son of German-Jewish immigrants and all he was doing. In fact, he had grown to like Germany so much he decided to stay on as a civilian, doing the same kind of work he did in the Army, helping nurture the postwar German economy and revive the country's democratic spirit. He

didn't move back to the States till the mid-fifties. He settled
down in the Washington, D.C., area where he eventually went on
to be a prominent government attorney. He is still an avid supporter of the Army's Civil Affairs program, though he is critical
of the lack of education and training for today's CA troops.

"The people I served with in Germany were really the best,
smartest people our country could come up with: there were engineers, economists, administrators, lawyers, all the best in their
field, and all fluent in German." Back then, he said, Americans
were proud, unabashed nation-builders: remaking the world in
our own freewheeling, prosperous image was considered only
natural, for a nation that considered itself the crowning achieve-
ment of the human race and a model for other less-fortunate
lands.

More recently, both Army and Marine troops did a tremen-
dous amount of CA type work in Vietnam, funding orphanages,
teaching school, introducing hybrid "miracle rice" seeds, running medical clinics in villages and paving roads. It wasn't called
"Civil Affairs." The South Vietnamese were our allies, and officially Civil Affairs operates only in occupied or conquered land,
so most of the overall aid effort, known as CORDS (Civil Operations and Revolutionary Development Support), was under
nominally civilian control; still, military officers like the contro-
versial Col. Paul Vann, made famous in David Halberstam's
book *The Best and the Brightest,* played a leading role in shaping
the programs and lobbying for more support for them.

Some military historians today think the Vietnam War could
have been won if the Marines' early Strategic Enclave strategy, in
which Leathernecks and local Vietnamese villagers worked together to create secure enclaves, had been given more of a

chance, along with the CORDS programs. Instead, the Marine and Army officers who favored the CA-style approach were gradually shunted aside in favor of Gen. William Westmoreland's "Total War" approach, which ended up devastating the country it was supposed to be saving.

A few outspoken officers have begun voicing fears that we may be heading down the same path in Iraq today, pointing to the recent operation in Fallujah as a classic example of "We had to destroy the village in order to save it." Of course, our military has made great strides in combat efficiency in the years following Vietnam: in the case of Fallujah, it took us only a few days to annihilate an entire city.

3

IN THE PAST few years, we have found ourselves in a peculiar kind of global conflict, which we call the War on Terrorism, but in which the real foes are poverty, disorder and inchoate violence, smoldering and igniting in dysfunctional failed nation-states and anarchic No-Man's-Lands, and leaping imaginary borders and porous frontiers like the airborne flames of a brushfire in a high wind. In this worldwide free-fire zone it is becoming increasingly clear that there are no rear areas or secure fortresses. Ground Zero is literally everywhere.

During this same period of time, the United States military has found itself, through no choice of its own, both the main executor of American foreign policy and the sole real guarantor of world order; all this, while facing the dizzy new reality of violence and misery that cannot be contained through force alone.

This Third World War of ours cannot be won with cruise missiles, stealth aircraft, smart bombs and fleets of aircraft carriers. Potential enemies are just too numerous, anonymous and resourceful; factor in the equations of assymetrical warfare and everyman becomes Attila the Hun, able to lay waste the civilized world with a stroke of his sword. Consider the impact an apparent lone crank armed with a few weapons-grade anthrax had on

our nation; a bona-fide terror group with a kilogram of the stuff
and an intelligent plan of attack could have totally shut down the
country for weeks—no mail, no travel, no public meetings or in-
terstate trucking—triggering a global depression.

It seems almost miraculously serendipitous that our armed
forces have just the right weapon to win this new kind of war:
Civil Affairs troops, with their nation-building, repairing and
stabilizing skills. The range of problems they are trained to deal
with is awesome: public administration, education, public
health, law, order and justice, business and trade, agriculture
and food supply, communication, public utilities, roads,
refugees, art and culture, the media, disaster management and
environmental protection. "I think they do windows, too," one
CA insider has commented wryly. They are already being deployed all over the world, in countries ranging from Afghanistan,
Iraq and Somalia to Kosovo, Colombia and Honduras, helping
hold things together.

All this being so, you would think Civil Affairs would be on
the very top when our military planners go through their pile of
current and present dangers, crises and emergencies. But no: on
the contrary, CA remains "the Pentagon's bastard stepchild," in
the words of one CA officer I met in Iraq. Its techniques and tac-
tics are not covered in the course curriculum at West Point, and
no West Point graduate has ever chosen CA as a career path: it is
considered the deadest of dead ends on the officer track.

There are fewer than five thousand troops in all of
UCAPOC(A), the U.S. Army Civil Affairs and Psychological
Operations Command (Airborne), and 97 percent of them are
reservists, part-time soldiers, members of twenty-four battalions
based the length and breadth of the United States. (There is also

a single full-time regular Army CA battalion, the 96th, headquartered at Fort Bragg; it has approximately 250 members.)

Its reserve character, with its mingling of military and civilian skills, is CA's unique strength. CA reservists include EMTs, cops, schoolteachers, judges, engineers, carpenters, doctors and nurses, farmers, firemen, bankers and business executives. Like one of those giant Swiss Army knives, CA can come up with a tool for just about any nation-building task. But the same preponderance of reservists in CA also contributes to its most glaring weakness—its lack of manpower: not only are CA troops few in number, only the 3 percent in the 96th are available for duty full-time. Overdeployed and underpaid, exhausted by endless rounds of missions, our CA soldiers are stretched to the limit today, and it is going to get worse, not better, as more and more trouble spots pop up around the planet.

We are barely holding the line in the struggle against chaos and the terror it breeds; without Civil Affairs, we might well be in full retreat. To paraphrase Winston Churchill, "Never have so many depended for so much on so few."

PART II

INTO IRAQ

4

I HAVE ALWAYS been leery of war correspondents who live in hotels with other journalists and drop in on military units for a few days at a time: in all too many cases it produces a kind of journalstic groupthink, in which reporters cobble together a version of the situation they are all comfortable with, and then ring up variations on it in the field. When the United States invaded Iraq, the journalistic pack leaned toward glorifying our military successes while shrugging off civilian casualties, collateral damage and the other harsh realities of warfare. Now what little reporting there was out of Iraq presented the war of occupation and counterinsurgency as a random series of assassinations, firefights and explosions. If there was an overall picture, it was a vague and blurry impression of gloom and doom, maybe accurate but without much substance.

Now that I had spent time with the 489th in Afghanistan, I wanted to see more of Civil Affairs in action, and it was clear that this meant going to Iraq. That was where push was coming to shove, for the U.S. military in general and CA in particular; all the other Civil Affairs missions around the world were really sideshows. Iraq was also where CA was facing the biggest challenges in its long history.

Afghanistan had been a comparatively easy proposition. It was essentially a preindustrial society with a simple rural-based economy, just the kind of place for small CA teams operating on the grassroots level. In addition, the Afghan people were heartily sick of the Taliban by the time we intervened, and the country had been so devastated for so long that any aid made for dramatic improvements. There were still potential enemies, especially in the old hard-core Taliban heartland around the Khyber Pass and south of Kandahar, but even there most Afghans seemed to be sick of fighting after nearly three decades of war, and seemed willing to give the Americans a chance to prove themselves.

Iraq was a whole other ball game. A majority of Iraqis, especially the Shi'ites and Kurds, may have been glad to see Saddam go, but that didn't mean they were thrilled to have his regime replaced by an army of Crusaders, infidels, few of whom could say as much as "Howdy" or "Sorry I blew up your date palms" in Arabic. Not only that, Iraq was a modern, industrialized nation-state, with big Western-style cities, freeways, television and traffic jams. It had the highest literacy rate in the Islamic Middle East, and up until the disastrous war with Iran, the invasion of Kuwait and the subsequent postwar sanctions, it had been extremely prosperous, with a large, rapidly growing middle class. Back in those golden years before Saddam began squandering the country's wealth on wars and weapons, the Iraqi dinar was the most stable currency in the entire region: even the citizens of wealthy oil sheikhdoms like Kuwait and the United Arab Emirates preferred to keep their savings in dinars rather than their own countries' money.

Quite simply, Iraq had had farther to fall than Afghanistan, and as of 2003 it had definitely hit the bottom, with the American intervention finishing everything off. The heavy industries had been bombed out or gutted by looters, there were hundreds of thousands of unemployed ex-soldiers wandering the streets, and the infrastructure, already in sorry shape due to years of sanctions, had been all but put out of commission in the fighting; water, sewage and electrical systems were crumbling, highways were falling apart, hospitals lacked basic equipment and medical supplies, and many schools had been damaged, looted or were in areas where it was just too dangerous for children to attend. CA had a huge task before them in Iraq, a veritable mountain of problems to overcome.

There was another way in which Iraq was unique as far as Civil Affairs was concerned. In every other war involving CA troops, they had played a subsidiary role: combat arms units, artillery, armor infantry, air power and the rest fought the main event, and CA was on the undercard. But in Phase Two of the Iraq War, occupation and rebuilding versus insurrection and terrorism, CA troops were at least as important as the gunslingers and cannon-cockers. It is no exagerration to say that by its successes or failures CA could either win or lose the Iraq War.

There was no way some fly-by-night tour, choppering from one CA team to the next with a Public Affairs officer telling me what I was seeing, would do justice to the story of Civil Affairs in Iraq. I would have to live with one small team, similar to the Chiclets in Afghanistan, long-term, 24/7, for several months.

When the first U.S. troops entered Baghdad in April 2003, Civil Affairs soldiers were among them: Col. Robert Frame and a team from the College Park, Maryland–based 350th CA Battalion, there to help get the Iraqi capital's hospitals back up and

running. Colonel Frame, a slight, wiry, unassuming fellow who
is a maxillofacial surgeon in civilian life, had led a team on the
same kind of mission in Kabul when the U.S. liberated
Afghanistan two years before, and they had succeeded in getting
the city's medical services back in gear after only a few months.
Colonel Frame had loved working with Afghan doctors and
nurses, and he looked forward to the challenge of doing the
same kind of gratifying work in postwar Baghdad.

A couple of weeks after they arrived in Iraq, Colonel Frame
and several fellow CA soldiers and Iraqi assistants attended a
meeting with ministers of the old regime at the Ministry of
Health. He and his companions had just left the ministry compound when ambushers hiding in a crowd opened up on their
two Humvees with AK-47s; someone inside the ministry had
probably tipped them off, told them the Americans were coming. Everyone in Frame's vehicle was hit; the driver took a bullet
above his body armor that entered high on his chest and exited
his lower back. Colonel Frame covered his wounded comrade
with his body, taking several bullets in his protective armor as he
and the others in the Humvees returned fire. One slug hit Frame
in his right forearm, virtually shattering it. All the Americans and
their Iraqi friends miraculously survived, and they managed to
kill all their assailants without hitting anyone else in the crowd.

After he was medevacked to the United States, Colonel
Frame underwent seven operations on his injured arm. When I
met him in January 2004, a couple of weeks before I left for Iraq,
he had just been told he would never regain the full use of his
right arm: for all intents and purposes, his career as a surgeon
was over. Surprisingly, he didn't seem at all bitter; in fact, he told

me he really wanted to go back to Iraq someday and do more medical aid work to help the people there.

Since that first incident, many CA soldiers serving in Iraq have been wounded or killed. Spec. Mark Anthony Bibby of the Greensboro, North Carolina 422nd CA Battalion, for example: just twenty-six years old, he had recently gone back to school and was a sophomore at North Carolina A&T. His job in Iraq was detecting and decontaminating nuclear, biological and chemical weapons, to safeguard his fellow CA soldiers and the Iraqis they were trying to help. On July 21, 2003, Bibby was killed when his team was ambushed while on its way to repair a water treatment plant outside Baghdad. Just before I left for Iraq, nineteen-year-old Spec. Nichole Frye of the 415th, who had been dreaming of a career in forest firefighting back home in Wisconsin, was killed when a command-detonated IED mangled the Humvee she was driving in Baquba, north of Baghdad. She had been in-country only two weeks.

Still, the work has continued without interruption. In the outlaw town of Ar Rutbah near the Jordanian border, troops from the Staten Island–based 304th CA Battalion and Philadelphia's 353rd ended up having to pacify the lawless place themselves before they could start their rebuilding mission. Ar Rutbah was once a busy truckers' stop on the road from Iraq into Jordan; it was the only real town in the province, surrounded by desert grazing lands populated by Bedouin nomads, and war and decreased trade had left it a virtual ghost town. Saddam Hussein's regime had given up delivering aid to the area in 1990, and everything—electricity, medical care, even food and water— was in short supply. The roads were disintegrating into rubble.

Aid delivered across the border from Jordan had helped the people of Ar Rutbah survive, but now with the frontier closed and bandits moving freely in the postwar chaos, traffic had slowed to a trickle.

When M. Sgt. Joe Rodriguez and his small team from the 304th arrived in Ar Rutbah, the place looked like a machine-age archeological site. People glared from crumbling doorways, eye-sniping the American soldiers; their faces were tight with anger, hunger, suspicion. Everything man-made was either rusting away, falling down or broken into pieces. Rodriguez had seen more than his share of miserable places years ago as a young Marine in Vietnam, but this was post-apocalyptic.

The people of Ar Rutbah were a tough lot: they had survived the last decade by smuggling and stealing, and they hated and distrusted outsiders. Anti-American fedayeen were already operating in the desert outside the town, sniping at American convoys and checkposts; some were undoubtedly from Ar Rutbah, members of the same community the Americans had come to help.

The members of the 304th and 353rd had to rely on their urban street smarts as well as their military training to carry out their mission and not get zapped or dinged, killed or wounded, doing it. One of their first missions was escorting a truckload of food and hospital equipment from the border through bandit country to Ar Rutbah. The truck made it through safely, and was greeted by a smiling, ebullient local in sunglasses and spotless *dishdashas* (robes), claiming to be the mayor and offering to take charge of the shipment.

Maj. Mike Kupchick and Capt. Mark Baaden, who were in charge of the aid delivery, were cops in civilian life, Kupchick

with the DEA and Baaden with the New York State Highway Patrol; when it came to monkey business, they'd seen it all. They
quickly unmasked the "mayor" as a fake, found the real mayor
and handed over custody of the aid cargo to him. A half hour
later they checked and found that the truck had disappeared.
"Ar Rutbah is our beat now," Baaden said later. "We know it the
same as we do the streets back home." They found the truck un-
loading its cargo at the mayor's private warehouse. After a brief
confab—the mayor claimed he had "misunderstood" the soldiers' directions—the truck was finally rerouted to its original
destination, the local hospital. The locals gathered there actually
cheered the two Americans as the precious cargo was unloaded.

Baaden and Kupchick's interpreter was a young former
schoolteacher named Sayeed; when asked how he felt about the
Americans, he exclaimed, "The mayor wanted electricity, and
we got electricity. The mayor wanted water, and we got water.
Mike and Mark are good! America is good!" When the fedayeen
in the area planned an operation, someone passed the word on to
Sayeed, who then warned the Civil Affairs troops.

Elsewhere in Iraq, thirty-year-old Sgt. Glen Corliss of the
353rd CA Battalion toiled almost single-handedly to salvage the
country's heavy industries. Formerly subsidized by Saddam's
regime, they were classic state-run enterprises, corrupt, ineffi-
cient and primitive; now, with the damage from the war and the
looting, most of them were either totally closed down or barely
operating, leaving hundreds of thousands of workers unemployed. Corliss was perfect for the job of trying to save them: an
investment planner on Wall Street in civilian life, he had enlisted
in the Army Reserves immediately after 9/11.

Over the next fifteen months Corliss inspected defunct factories, repaired or replaced broken machinery, coached managers on the importance of everything from consumer demand to accurate inventories and accounting, and searched for foreign investors to fund needed improvements. He also found time to run a program that taught over five thousand Iraqis how to start up their own businesses.

Capt. Stacey Simms of Greensboro, North Carolina's 422nd CA Battalion, also arrived in Iraq with the first wave of CA troops. He spent every spare minute roaming the back streets of Baghdad, searching out orphaned and abandoned street kids. At first these damaged children were wary, even frightened, of the big African-American soldier in the dark glasses and strange uniform, but in time he became a familiar figure they knew and trusted. He took them back to the 422nd's post, gave them a square meal and then found a local orphanage with room for them. Some of the orphanages he visited were in bad shape, their buildings damaged and furniture stolen by looters and their funds exhausted. Captain Simms passed the hat among his fellow soldiers, paid for the most immediate needs and put the needy orphanages in touch with NGOs who could provide long-term funding and support. All of this was in addition to his work on the battalion's assigned missions.

A CA team in Baghdad rescued the city petting zoo's animals, which were dying of starvation, disease and thirst. After providing emergency food and water, they arranged for the animals to be adopted by foreign aid aid workers. Another team east of Baghdad discovered the local farmers had no way of getting their crops to the markets downtown. They found a group of truckers who needed work and got them the necessary passes

and permits to travel to and from the capital. Then they helped
the farmers form an agricultural co-op, to transport and sell their
produce collectively. Now the farmers were getting paid for their
crops, the truckers had work, and urban Iraqis were able to buy
fresh fruit and vegetables every day in the bazaar.

Our Civil Affairs soldiers had racked up some impressive
successes in Iraq, despite all the difficulties. At the same time,
the news reports out of there in the weeks before my departure
painted an increasingly bleak picture of ever-widening and
deepening anarchy and insurrection.

I would be searching for answers to several questions in Iraq.
Were there enough CA troops there to do the job? If not, and if
as a result the situation in Iraq was deteriorating, were we approaching a tipping point where effective Civil Affairs work itself
would become impossible due to the level of violence? Or was
Civil Affairs, always remarkable for its ability to adapt on the fly,
still finding ways to operate? Would the nation-building process
take hold while there was still an Iraqi nation left to work on, or
would the whole edifice shatter into a mosaic of warfare, every
sect and ethnicity for itself and the United States against all, until we finally ran out of faith and will and abandoned Iraq and
along with it our role as the guardian of orderly progress in the
world?

Or, to put it more bluntly, would we lose the war for Iraq,
and the greater War on Terrorism along with it? It seemed to
me that the fate of Civil Affairs in Iraq was inextricably tangled
up with these questions and how they would be answered in
the end.

5

I ARRIVE IN Baghdad on a C-130 transport from Kuwait. The last twenty minutes before we land at BIAP the plane goes through a series of wild evasive maneuvers, sideslipping, diving, porpoising. A few months ago the insurgents fired a SAM and hit a big cargo jet two miles above Baghdad; the plane managed to land safely, but the Bad Guys will no doubt try again. Flight crewmen peer out the C-130's bubble windows, watching for missile vapor trails, and the plane spews metallic chaff and flares in its wake to spoof heat-seeking warheads and radar. Finally we touch down, decelerate and taxi over to the passenger terminal, a sandbagged encampment of tents and Quonset huts.

My first view of Iraq is unprepossessing. In the distance, across the vast expanse of runways, the main terminal buildings, offices and warehouses shimmer in the heat: here and there are signs of bomb damage, collapsed roofs, blownout windows, fractured walls. Gunships and transport choppers sit in long rows; their drooping rotor blades give them an exhausted air. Tents, dust, heavy machinery, armor, industrial trash, chain link and razor wire, Humvees, dust and more dust—an ugly, in-your-face scene. The horizon consists of dusty palm trees and flat roofs, with a few mosque domes sprouting like toadstools.

In most Islamic countries, mosques are architectural masterpieces, islands of celestial beauty that bring a note of otherworldly grace to the everyday landscape, but not here in Iraq. With comparatively few exceptions the mosques of Baghdad are soulless ultramodern affairs, totally lacking in conviction or vision, built by Saddam's regime to advertise the Maximum Leader's ersatz piety. They are humongous sprawling structures of pre-stressed concrete, bristling with spires that look strangely like missiles or spaceships, and smaller gingerbread temples, clumsy and garish, worsened by tacky decorative tilework.

I have been invited to Iraq by Lt. Col. Sean Kelly, CO of the 425th Civil Affairs Battalion, based in Santa Barbara, California. During my research, I have gotten to know some of the leading lights in the CA community, including retired Gen. Dennis Wilkie, an immensely hospitable, learned gentleman who knows more about CA than any other living person, and Gen. Herbert "Buzz" Altshuler, the current commandant of USACAPOC at Bragg. Thanks to them, I received a blanket invitation to go to Iraq with any one of the CA battalions being sent there. When Colonel Kelly and the 425th arrived at Fort Bragg for last-minute training before leaving for Iraq, someone there told Kelly about my project, and he was curious enough to Google me on his laptop. Evidently my years of reporting from Afghanistan and the *Time* magazine article I had written about Chiclet-5's exploits in Afghanistan reassured him that I was okay, and he decided it would be"interesting" to have an outsider with the battalion in Iraq, to get a civilian perspective on how the missions went. Just before Christmas 2003 he phoned me up from Bragg, introduced himself and asked if I wanted to fly over with him and his troops in three or four weeks. I thought about it for about five seconds, and said yes.

In the end, the 425th actually beat me to Baghdad by two weeks. The battalion had saved a seat for me on the flight over to Kuwait from Pope AFB, Fort Bragg's air transport hub, but at the last second the Army's notorious bureaucracy foiled the plan. CENTCOM, the Tampa, Florida–based military command for the Middle East, never bothered to fill out the necessary paperwork to get me on the plane; they also neglected to tell me about their error of omission. The flight was scheduled to depart Pope on Super Bowl Sunday; I drove down to Fayetteville the day before, packed up and raring to go, only to find that I couldn't get on the plane. The 425th flew out with one empty seat, and I ended up spending another couple of weeks buying a ticket and getting a transit visa for Kuwait. A series of three commercial flights took me from Washington, D.C., to London to Dubai to Kuwait, where I finally caught a military shuttle to BIAP.

The 425th is based right here at the airport: the battalion TOC is over by the PX and the red and white circus-style tent named for Bob Hope that houses the main mess hall, and the members of the battalion are scattered all over BIAP and beyond. Eventually all the thousands of servicemen and women housed here will move over to Camp Victory, a giant dust-bowl trailer camp that is going in next to the airport; for the time being, this is home to the 425th and dozens of other MP, Special Forces, 1st Armored Division, Delta Force, transport, payroll and clerical, intelligence and commo, Air Force and everything-else-under-the-sun units.

I end up settling in with the 425th's Public Health Team, in a bunkhouse-style building that formerly housed Republican Guards on airport security duty. Most of the battalion's Alpha Company is living in the same area, a weird zone of canals, artificial lakes and tall banks of papyrus reeds. The buildings here are similarly surreal, including imitation Greek temples with ornamental columns, shabby miniature beach houses overlooking the water, utilitarian blockhouses and crapped-out Third World office clumps.

Here at the airport you can barely tell you are in Iraq at all, mainly because you really aren't. Iraq is outside, beyond the razor wire and the walls; everything inside has been transformed into a weird kind of jerry-built military-colonial Semi-America, the USA in khaki and cammo. The Bob Hope Defac serves cheeseburgers, pizzas, salad-bar salads and entrées like baked chicken, spaghetti and pot roast, while huge TV screens on the walls show college football, NBA basketball and FOX News, and if someone wants an all-American snack between their all-American meals there is a Burger King next to the PX. At night, people put on headphones or glue themselves to portable DVD players or TVs and cocoon themselves in American pop culture.

Everywhere you look are Americans in uniform, carrying weapons, M-16s and 9mm pistols, riding in Humvees, Bradley fighting vehicles, Abrams tanks, Mk-113 armored personnel carriers, fuel tankers and tractor-trailer HETs. The only Iraqis around are service workers, driving garbage trucks, emptying the hundreds of plastic ToiFor outhouses and building roads and barricades under the watchful eyes and guns of American soldiers. You could live and work at BIAP for a year and never really leave home. It's a strange place to find CA soldiers, a far, far

cry from Bamiyan, where Colonel Walker and his men were totally immersed in Afghanistan, 24/7, whether they liked it or not.

After a few days I begin to suss out what has happened here.
During the first few months of the U.S. occupation, things were
comparatively mellow. In the immediate aftermath of Saddam's
ouster, most Iraqis were willing to give their new caretakers a
chance, and those who weren't were lying low, cowed by the
speed and the overwhelming force of the American victory.
Many Coalition advisors and officials lived outside the Green
Zone and the other bases and compounds, in rented houses and
apartments; they commuted to work in civilian vehicles, and
mingled with everyday Iraqis at shops, cafes and restaurants.

But as time went by, more and more Iraqis became restive at
the slow pace of reconstruction and the CPA's adamant refusal
to include unemployed ex-soldiers and Ba'ath Party members in
the new national administration. The disenfranchised Iraqis began to regroup in opposition to the foreign invaders, along with
Iraqis who just plain didn't want infidels in their homeland.

Simultaneously, foreign terrorists, jihadists and agents from
unfriendly countries like Iran began to arrive with money, arms
and expertise in guerrilla warfare. In the months before I arrived, attacks on allied soldiers and civilians and their Iraqi comrades had greatly increased.

The U.S. military has already tightened up security protocols in response to the increased dangers. In effect, our occupation authority here, both civilian and military, is pulling back
into its shell and greatly reducing contacts beteen the U.S. military and the Iraqi people. If the process isn't reversed, there will

be an airtight wall between the Americans and the Iraqis before long.

Already, friendly Iraqis are complaining that their only contacts with their self-described "liberators" are armed convoys speeding through their neighborhoods, running local drivers off the road, and checkpoints where they are shouted at and roughed up by fearful, hostile soldiers.

Of course, all this makes CA work really difficult. In the words of one 425th officer, "Civil Affairs is sticky business. You have to get close to the people you are working with, get to know them, live alongside them. That's the only way you can change hearts and minds."

I end up spending my first month going out with the Public Health Team. They are a great bunch, and they are definitely making the best of a tough situation. Col. Steve "Doc" Watters is a middle-aged veterinary surgeon who has pulled CA missions from Southeast Asia to the Balkans, doing everything from inoculating elephants in Laos to helping Bosnian shepherds crossbreed their flocks to make them stronger and more productive. I think of him as Dr. Dolittle in uniform: his sole interest in coming to Iraq is to heal animals and help people. Others in the battalion tell me that a few years ago Doc's only son died suddenly of a freak cerebral hemorrhage. In the aftermath of the tragedy his wife left him and his vet business folded. For years his friends never saw him smile. A few months ago he and a woman who works in his new veterinary clinic fell in love, and he is learning to be happy again. He shows photographs of the woman to everyone he meets: her face radiates the same kind of kindness I see in Doc's.

The team's other vet, Colonel Lumberg, is a hulking

Pithecanthropine character; unlike the soft-spoken Watters, he is full of loud and unabashed American patriotism. His specialty is big cats; zoos all over the world fly him in to operate on their lions, tigers and leopards. He has a full-grown pet Bengal tiger back home on his ranch in Colorado; the beast runs free there, chasing after Lumberg like a two-thousand-pound tabby when he works his fields in his tractor.

Lt. Darrow "El Tee" Dickey joined the Army reserves at the advanced age of forty-one. He works as a SAG card–carrying stunt man back in Hollywood, a job he describes as "falling out of things, crashing into things, and fighting"; he has also fought in nearly fifty no-holds-barred Tough Man boxing competitions and runs a small custom printing business with the twee name "Dickey Bird Productions." He has a degree in Civil Engineering to boot, and can diagnose a dead generator or design a sewer system on the spot. Doc Lee, the youthful energetic battalion MD, is an emergency room physician back in southern California.

The team gets its vital combat skills and street smarts from Sgt. Tommy Borton, a skinny little Kentuckian with a mischievous Huck Finn–style sense of humor. An ex-Ranger, veteran of the Mogadishu Convoy (the one immortalized in *Black Hawk Down*), a career soldier who salutes in his sleep and bleeds OD, Tommy is a pure product of that same kickass American country breed an Audie Murphy and Sergeant York with an attitude as hard as woodpecker lips. In Civil Affairs units, good ones at least, function overrules form, skill trumps rank and brass bows to battlefield experience. There are two lieutenant colonels on the PH Team, not to mention a first lieutenant, but Sergeant Borton is the unquestioned combat leader, the one to listen to when the shit hits the fan and the bullets fly.

The PHT's mission list is absurdly large. They are supposed to keep Baghdad's hospitals and clinics up and running, reopen the big veterinary college north of BIAP and reinstate inoculation programs for Iraqi livestock; the Tigris-Euphrates Valley is such an unhealthy place for domestic animals that when the Saddam regime imported a herd of water buffalo from India they all promptly died. The PH Team is also tasked to modernize slaughterhouses and food processing plants, help Iraqi MDs edit and publish the *Journal of Iraqi Medicine,* and troubleshoot public health problems like broken or nonexistent sewer systems and unsanitary open-air garbage dumps.

As if all that wasn't way too much, another job was tossed in their lap when they arrived in Iraq: help to reopen the Baghdad Zoo by rehabbing sick and injured animals and cleaning up the facilities. Some genius at the Coalition Provisional Authority has decided that what Iraqis need is a fully functioning national zoo: this in a country with a shattered infrastructure, 60 percent unemployment and an incipient civil war. One CA officer refers to the project as "polishing brasswork on the *Titanic.*" Theirs not to reason why, though: these guys may joke sometimes about the idiocy of the orders their superiors pass down, but then they just lower their heads and keep pushing the missions.

I ride along as Doc Watters and company zoom from place to place and job to job. One day they are checking on a clinic way out in the farming country outside Baghdad, where the people, descendants of the very first agriculturalists, have been working the same swatches of earth for eons, a primeval world of palm trees, muddy canals, mud walls and robed figures riding donkeys. The next day they are meeting with civilian bureaucrats in an air-conditioned office in the Green Zone, trying to make sense of their grandiose plans and inscrutable jargon. Then they are back in northeastern Baghdad, along a freeway, listening to locals report that an American convoy just ran over a little girl and left her lying in the road; they show us skid marks and a pool of bright red blood. Then we are at a women's clinic in a wealthy downtown neighborhood; then the hospital we checked on my first day with the team; then Iraq's one and only pig farm, where an old Christian veterinarian produces pork roasts and chops for Baghdad's small non-Moslem community; then an open trash dump in the miserable town of Abu Ghraib, just north of the airport, where children play in raw sewage, rotting animal carcasses and rusty metal.

The PHT guys are doing a great job, identifying problems and either taking care of them or kicking them up the line to be solved, but it is ultimately frustrating. The team members never really get to know the people they are helping, or see the results of their work. If CA is supposed to be "sticky business," you need enough time for the stickiness to take hold. The PHT soldiers aren't the only members of the battalion facing this problem.

There is one notable exception among the 425th troops stationed at BIAP: M.Sgt. Bob Venters, who is in charge of the A-LOC, Alpha Company's headquarters compound down the road from the Public Health Team's house. Venters is a pleasant-faced old soldier who fought in Vietnam and later was middle-weight Army boxing champion in Europe; in civilian life he has worked as a martial arts instructor and a deputy sheriff in rural Washington State. He and his wife have a half dozen kids, and there are usually four or five more teenagers and adolescents liv-

ing with them, outcasts from broken violent homes or whose
families don't want them.

Like so many authentic warriors, Venters is a compassionate
man. He isn't even supposed to be aiding Iraqis—his job is logistics, housing, all the day-to-day work of keeping a company
functioning—but he has befriended the Iraqi workers who are
repairing and cleaning the A-LOC and other battalion buildings,
and helping them and their families has followed naturally. Venters's hooch literally overhangs one of the ornamental lagoons
that mottle this part of the airport: step out his back door, and
you would fall six feet straight down into the water. Every evening he sits on his roof and fishes for the big carp that lurk in the
muddy waters below, and the first thing each morning he distributes his catch among the Iraqi workers. To them, this is like a
bona-fide miracle: soldiers are supposed to be hard and cruel,
like Saddam's Republican Guards, and carp are special, food for
feasts and celebrations, and this conquering infidel is giving
them away for free with a smile on his face.

Venters has taken a particular interest in one of the Iraqis,
Hamid, a well-spoken older man with an engineering degree
who supervises most of the work. One of Hamid's daughters
has MS and, by coincidence, so does one of Venters's sons. In
another coincidence, one of Venters's Vietnam buddies, another
old CA sergeant, was stationed here before the 425th arrived and
he had already been helping Hamid and his daughter before
Venters got here. "Under Saddam, my daughter didn't even have
a wheelchair," Hamid tells me. "Now she has two." The sergeants had them airfreighted from the States. Inspired by the
movie *My Left Foot*, Venters taught his son to draw with a pencil
in his mouth; now he has bought art supplies for Hamid's

daughter, and she has been producing drawings with the fervor of someone who has been longing to express herself throughout her life but never could. "She's really good, too—I mean she's special," Sergeant Venters says proudly. "I'd like to set up a show of her drawings here, or maybe back in the States." He shows me slides of the girl, a frail birdlike wraith with a megawatt smile, and of her art: precise renditions of Baghdad— buildings, streets and trees—diamond-bright and ineluctable.

The thought strikes me that maybe this is why we invaded Iraq, the secret reason behind the war: so that good ol' Sergeant Venters can change the life of one little girl, and hand out fish to a bunch of workers. It makes a lot more sense at this point than all the official illusions, like finding weapons that aren't there, or building mansions on sand and castles in the air.

The PH Team's interpreters, call them Ron and Mickey, are the first Iraqis I really get to know well. Ron, a big, chubby, ebullient Shi'a kid, is majoring in computer science at Baghdad University; he would fit right in on the UCLA campus or in the office of a Silicon Valley startup. Mickey, a Sunni Moslem originally from Mosul in northern Iraq, is older, short and slight, with a small mustache; his weary, worldly smile says he has seen it all before, and what he saw was pretty damned unappealing. In time I will discover that beneath his cool facade Mickey is a complete romantic idealist. In addition to helping the PH Team, he works nights as an undercover agent for Army Military Intelligence, helping track down terrorists and arms. He has been repeatedly threatened with death by the insurgents, and sometimes he doesn't go home to his wife and children in east Baghdad for days, even weeks, sleeping in his car or at friends' houses: he reasons that the Bad Guys won't kill his family unless he is there, too. The two men worked as a team interpreting for the Marines during the march on Baghdad and have been together ever since. Ron and Mickey are not employees as much as they are members of the PH Team: they don't only translate words; they tell the Americans what Iraqis are really thinking, and they advise the team on everything from how to avoid danger around the next corner to what's happening day to day in the streets across Iraq.

Doc Watters especially likes talking with Mickey, and one day he vents about a hospital the team just visited, where a previous CA team had made a whole lot of glorious promises and not fulfilled any of them. It's not the first such case the PH Team has encountered, where someone in an American uniform promised Iraqis the moon and then vanished, never to be seen again.

"The first rule in CA work is, never make a promise you can't keep," Doc tells Mickey. "Once you lose the people's trust, you never get it back. And we're starting to run into broken promises all over the place. No wonder people are shooting at us."

"You're right, Dr. Watters," Mickey agrees. "Many, many Iraqis were so happy and full of hope when the Americans first came here; they thought America can do anything—after all, you are the only superpower in the world. But now people I know are saying, 'What is this America? Even Saddam was better.' After the war with Kuwait, and the Iran-Iraq War too, the destruction was much worse, but everything was rebuilt in six months."

"What do *you* think?" Doc Watters asks.

One of Mickey's best attributes is his honesty: he isn't afraid to tell us the truth, even if it has a bitter taste. "A lot of the time I think the same way. I look around, and nothing has really changed since you came here and got rid of Saddam. Everything is still broken, ruined, and you Americans don't seem to care."

Ron concurs. "Water, power, garbage everywhere—it didn't used to be like this. Baghdad was a modern city. Last summer when it was so hot, I would sit in my apartment at night, and I could have cooked an egg on the ceiling, I swear to you. I got so angry, I said, 'God damn these Americans. Why did they come here, anyway? To save us? Please, next time can you save someone else?' "

He, Mickey and Doc Watters all laugh.

"You know, there is a saying in Baghdad now," Mickey says. "The Americans always make the best choice, after they have tried all the other choices first."

No doubt about it, somebody out there doesn't like the job we Americans are doing. Every night salvos of mortars and/or rockets hit the airport and Camp Victory. One day, right around noon, rockets start hitting, and just keep coming. One explodes right on Sergeant Venters's front doorstep, pretty much wrecking the place; luckily he is at work over at the A-LOC, or he probably would have been killed.

Out on the streets it is far worse. One day the PHT people are handing out toys at a hospital downtown when somebody sees the parking lot outside emptying, Iraqis jumping in their cars and fleeing. One of the doctors tells the team a hit squad of jihadis is on its way there to kill the CA soldiers. They have to dump the rest of the toys and Irene it out of there. Afterward, they can't stop talking about how they disappointed the kids. "You should have seen their faces," Doc Watters says. "They looked so scared. They didn't know what was going on. It broke your heart."

I am leaving the PHT guys for a while, and joining up with one of the 425th's CATs, Civil Affairs Teams; they are similar to both the PHT here and the Chiclet team in Afghanistan in strength, seven or eight members, but like the latter they work in one geographic area, doing the full range of CA missions, dealing with infrastructure, governance, the economy, law and order, health, the whole nine hundred and ninety-nine yards. This team works in Abu Ghraib, the mean town just north of BIAP whose inhabitants have been regularly attacking both the airport and Camp Victory.

The 425th has done an enormous amount of Civil Affairs work there, and so did the 490th CA Battalion that was here before, but none of that seems to have had any impact: the people there still hate us. Military vehicles traveling the main highway in and out of the town are hit by IEDs and ambushes every week, and troops that go in there can expect to be attacked at any moment.

The mayor of Abu Ghraib, an old Ba'ath Party stalwart, has been clouding the picture by feeding the Army a whole skein of false leads on who his town's Bad Guys are. He wants to get rid of the Gypsies camped out in one of the neighborhood's vast fields of trash, reportedly because he wants the land cleared so he can rebuild the brothel and bootlegging complex he ran there for his Ba'ath Party friends back in the Saddam era.

With this in mind, he reportedly paid the Abu Ghraib village idiot to fire at Camp Victory from inside the Gypsy camp at night, so we would blame the Gypsies. One night the idiot threw eight grenades at an LP out beyond the wire; fortunately, he neg-

lected to pull the pins first, so the grenades didn't go off. Well, if
at first you don't succeed . . . The mayor drove the idiot out to
the Gypsy camp a few nights later, handed him an RPG and told
him to fire it at a guard tower. As the mayor drove away, the idiot
aimed and fired, but the weapon was pointed the wrong way.
The rocket barely missed the mayor and his car.

Unbelievably, one of the 1st Armored Division colonels fell
for the sham: a few days ago he assembled a posse of bulldozers
and ordered it to raze the Gypsy camp to the ground. Luckily
the operation was called off at the last minute when wiser parties
informed the colonel that you can't wipe out an entire civilian
community just because you think the inhabitants have been
shooting at you. Since then, the violence in Abu Ghraib has continued unabated.

I have met the guys on this CAT a couple of times, and
talked with them enough to really like them. Despite the hostile
turf they work, they are full of stories about the friendly Iraqi
kids they have encountered. "Whenever we stop somewhere,
there's a big crowd of kids, and Mark goes into his Jackie Chan
act," one of the soldiers says of the team's Korean-American
member. "He stands back there on the SAW-gun and waves to
the crowd, and everybody starts cheering and yelling for Jackie
Chan. Mark always wears dark glasses and this black balaclava
hiding his face. First he takes off the dark glasses, and the kids
go crazy. Then he pulls off his balaclava and pumps his fists in
the air, and the Iraqis start yelling, '*Jackie Chan! Jackie Chan!*'"

"There's this one little kid we always used to see along the
road, and he'd always wave to us and cheer," another soldier
tells me. "Then one day we stopped right next to him and got
out, and the little guy got so excited he just started bawling. I had

to go over and hug him and pat him on the back till he calmed down."

Despite those touchy-feely incidents, Abu Ghraib is a wreck of such enormous scope and scale it is really out of Civil Affairs's league. The roads are disintegrating, the town is awash in raw sewage, and the town's main industry, the Milk Factory, needs tens of millions of dollars in new machinery to get going again. In one neighborhood, wryly named the City of Gold, people live in houses made of cow manure; it smells like you think it would.

Abu Ghraib points up perhaps the biggest problem facing our effort in Iraq: the big stuff—disintegrating roads, power plants that repeatedly fail, water and sewage systems that barely function or don't even exist, factories bombed out or looted—are the kinds of things that require billions of dollars and big corporations experienced in infrastructure building and repair, and they just aren't getting done. Either the jobs haven't been funded or the companies who have gotten contracts haven't come through. "What we should have done in places like Abu Ghraib and Sadr City is just come in, paved the streets, put in sewer lines, fixed the power grid and given everyone air conditioners, TV sets, satellite dishes and computers hooked up to the Internet," a 1st Cav officer told me. "Who cares how much it cost? It would be cheaper than fighting these people. Shit, *buy* their loyalty, kill 'em with kindness. Why not? How much is an American soldier's life worth, anyhow?"

Inevitably the situation in Abu Ghraib worsens, despite all of the CAT's attempts to help the place. A brand-new girls' school the 490th built has its walls covered with death threats against Iraqis who work with the Americans. The headmistress tells the CA soldiers she was been threatened with assassination, and parents are afraid to send their daughters to school because of gangs who have been kidnapping schoolchildren and holding them for ransom. Outside the school, street kids taunt the soldiers with raised middle fingers and throat-cutting gestures.

An Army patrol is ambushed on its way home from Abu Ghraib at dawn, and suffers one soldier killed and two wounded. A half dozen of the Army's Iraqi interpreters are murdered in a single week, and mortar rounds continue to hit BIAP's outlying posts. The situation becomes so critical that the Army puts together an operation called Iron Promise. This is to be a final all-out attempt to quash the town's insurgents and terrorists once and for all, a massive armored sweep through the town by the 1st Cavalry Division, along with a platoon of Estonians and Iraqi National Guard troops; the 382nd Field Artillery will be firing illumination rounds from their big self-propelled guns at Victory, and the 91st Engineers will be along to defuse IEDs and booby traps. The CAT troops are coming along to take care of any civilian damage claims that might occur. All of this is Top Top Secret: we are told about it only a few hours before the operation is to kick off, and we are warned not to phone or e-mail anyone back home about it, in case the Bad Guys are listening in.

At eleven P.M. we are milling around the rally point inside Camp Victory when someone from one of the 425th's other teams comes running up. "I just got off the Internet with my wife, and she told me we've been on CNN for the last six hours!" He is laughing.

"Who's 'we'?"

"Iron Promise—the whole operation. I guess the whole world knows about it by now."

It turns out that some Army PAO in the Green Zone issued a *press release* on Iron Promise this morning, including all the details—who, how many, when, where and why. Well, so much for "surprising" the Bad Guys. (We are told later by Iraqi interpreters that they've known about the operation for two days; the people in Abu Ghraib told them they thought the raid was going to happen night before last.)

For better or worse, the operation kicks off. Three company-sized armored columns—Annihilator, Black Hawk, Cold Steel—and the platoon-sized Stone element (Estonian troops), M-1 Abrams tanks, Bradleys, M-113 APCs, trucks and Hummers rumble out into the night. PAVE-LOW helicopters swoop overhead like swift shadows, lightless and nearly silent. The ground shakes, and dust fills the air.

I am in the back of the number two M-113 armored personnel carrier in one of the columns, along with three members of the CAT and an Army photographer covering the mission for *Stars and Stripes*. You can't see anything out of the windowless cabin, just the driver's back and the legs of the M-60 machine-gunner who peers out the top hatch. The roar of the engine is deafening.

After an interminable jouncing, juddering journey, we stop to regroup out by the Milk Factory complex. The vehicles shut their engines down, and in the silence you can hear dogs howling and soldiers talking in low voices. We step out into the cool night air, and ask someone why we are stopped; we are told the column's lead element spotted an IED planted on the way into the town, three 155mm rockets rigged to a trip wire, and the Engineers are dismantling it.

Finally it is time to go again; scores of half-smoked ciga-
rettes fly into the darkness, hatches clank down, diesels gun up.
We climb back in the can, and a few seconds later we are roaring
at high speed across the fields, into Abu Ghraib.

We arrive to a surreal scene. The central plaza of town is
jammed with vehicles and soldiers, choppers hover low overhead, and airburst illumination rounds from the big guns at Victory exsanguinate a weird red glow across the sky, casting huge
shadows. But the town itself seems oblivious: there's not a soul
to be seen, and the houses are dark and silent. Except for a few
streetlights burning and a light-bulb glowing here and there in
someone's compound, you would think we were in an abandoned ghost town.

For their part, the Cav guys are great: POLITE, PROFESSIONAL,
AND PREPARED TO KILL, as their sign at Camp Victory proclaims.
Before I left the States, I saw news footage of American troops
behaving like Huns or storm troopers as they searched houses,
yelling and cursing at terrified families, breaking furniture and
punching prisoners. In one excruciating scene, a soldier slapped
a terrified little boy who wouldn't stop crying. But these soldiers
make me proud. They talk quietly to the Iraqis through their interpreter, smile at the children, apologize to the women for bothering them, joke with the men as they line them up and
photograph them for the file of potential terrorists. In one house,
a teenaged boy scowls as he prepares to have his picture taken,
and complains loudly and angrily about the "———— ————
Americans—why have they come here, anyway?" One of the
Cav guys nudges the interpreter and says, "Tell him we're making a book about the eligible young bachelors of Abu Ghraib,
and he's going to be in it." When the interp manages to translate

the concept into Arabic, the teenager actually cracks up, and when we leave he is still chuckling.

But when you get right down to it, Iron Promise without the element of surprise is really, in the words of one young CA wise guy, *Ironic Premise*. The Bad Guys are either long gone or hiding in plain sight. In one house, we find seven young men whose ID papers, irreproachably correct, claim they are blood brothers: odd, because they look like a veritable ethnic Rainbow Coalition, one the spitting image of a North African Berber, another Sudanese, a third Afghan, and so on. They are the damnedest band of brothers we've ever seen, that's for sure, but what can the Cav soldiers do? If you've got the right papers, you walk: That's the rule, and orders is orders. The al-Qaeda Brothers smirk as the soldiers record their supposed names and photograph them.

We are supposed to be going to sixty houses, but by five A.M. we have done just fourteen. After one more unsuccessful search, the major in charge of the team calls it a night, and Iron Promise packs it in. As we return to the plaza, troops are filing back from every direction to their vehicles. Score: zero suspects found, and one weapon, an antique shotgun, turned in voluntarily by its owner and promptly given back to him.

On the positive side, the civilian damage claims from the whole operation total approximately 75 cents: six screws bent when a balky garage door was pried open, and a padlock broken when the house's owner couldn't find the key. Too good to be true, so of course it isn't: we are getting back in the M-113 when a soldier comes running up and tells the CAT troops that a Bradley knocked down the main gate and front wall of the Abu Ghraib Pickle Factory. It seems that some troops detected "strange smells" coming from inside and thought the place was a bomb-making factory. The Bradley tried to nudge the locked gate open, but the driver overrevved the engine, taking out the gate and twenty feet of adjacent wall. The CAT soldiers will have to come back and pay off the Pickle Factory owner.

Over the next two weeks the attacks out of Abu Ghraib escalate. Fuel and supply convoys, traveling with insufficient force protection, are hit with RPGs, heavy machine guns, mortars and small arms. One convoy of fuel tanker trucks is virtually destroyed, with two American civilian drivers killed and one taken prisoner. When the Quick Reaction Force arrives, ambushers are already set up to attack it. A medevac helicopter is downed by a SAM-7, and the surviving crew members barely escape an insurgent mortar barrage before a rescue party can reach their downed chopper and whisk them away.

At least the Abu Ghraib problem is finally solved: with BIAP down to three days of fuel thanks to destroyed and delayed tanker convoys, the Army has had enough. No more Mr. Nice Guy, no more Civil Affairs. They trot out the big guns, the tanks and the helicopter gunships, and they virtually level the town.

PART III

CAT-A 13

6

BOTH THE PHT and the Abu Ghraib CAT are doing good work, but the latter is handicapped by their intractable AO, plus being based at Camp Victory, and the former by an almost impossible mission list. As a consequence, neither has been able to develop the kind of close relationship with Iraqis that the Chiclet-5 troops had with the Hazaras of Bamiyan Valley, and that is the essence of Civil Affairs in action. That kind of bonding produces the enduring changes that real, successful nation-building depends on, as in postwar Germany and Japan.

At this point, after two months in Baghdad, I am not sure this is even possible in Iraq. Because I'm not sure we're not losing the war here: I'm not sure we've provided enough security for Civil Affairs to operate effectively in, and by failing in that set off a downward spiral in which the failure to rebuild Iraq creates still more insecurity, and so on and so on. Worse, I wonder if what is happening here in Iraq isn't going to ultimately lose us the greater War on Terrorism, too. I agree with those who say we didn't have to come here—however evil he was, Saddam was no threat to us or anyone outside Iraq, and his iron rule at home didn't allow room for the likes of al-Qaeda—but now that we've made our war,

we have to win it. Unlike Vietnam, we can't just take our ball and
glove and go home; the seismic shocks of an American defeat in
Iraq would roll around and around the world, toppling whatever
order we have created since the Cold War ended and loosing a
nightmare of anarchy, high crime and disorder without borders.

Sometime during my peregrinations around Greater Baghdad with the Public Health Team, we had dropped in on the
425th's most far-flung unit, CAT-A 13, Civil Affairs Team number thirteen of Alpha Company. They are based at Banzai FOB
(Forwarding Operations Base), an old Iraqi Army Intelligence
installation on a promontory on the west bank of the Tigris
River, far up on the northwest edge of Baghdad.

It strikes me that I haven't seen them recently. In fact, they
hardly ever come to BIAP; they seem content to stay in al-
Khadimiyah, the sprawling neighborhood that is their AO, and
work with the people there. In fact, I have heard a couple of officers
around the 425th TOC mildly criticize their CO, Major Clark, for
being too independent and not enough of a battalion team player.

I remember the few hours the PH Team and I spent with
them. We walked through the old bazaar in al-Khadimiyah,
checking out some of Major Clark's plans for improving the
place, wending through the crowds, talking with merchants and
shoppers. Many of the stallkeepers knew the Major and his
troops: they greeted him by name, and several offered us dates,
samples of soft cheese, dolmas. The CAT-A 13 soldiers were
definitely on guard: the round-faced sergeant named Paul, something like that, was constantly on the radio with the soldiers back
at the Humvees, and there was a big Hispanic-looking kid with

an M-16 whose head was continually on a swivel, 360 degrees, watching everybody. At the same time, the team somehow looked relaxed, like this was just another day on the block.

At the time, they had reminded me of the Chiclets, how they went through the bazaar in Bamiyan, schmoozing with merchants, joking around with kids, while Groce stood at the corner with the far M-60, scoping everything out. The locals had offered the CA troops food there, too; in fact, we had ended up eating lunch with one of the mission contractors in the back of his shop.

Somehow, Major Clark and his team seemed to have transcended the current situation, with its stringent Rules of Engagement and security protocols, and gotten close to the Iraqis they worked among. It probably helped that they were deployed far from the flagpole, away from the rule-makers and REMF regulation-freaks; but however they were doing it, they were doing it.

I don't know why I haven't thought of it before, but now I decide to try and join up with the CAT-A 13 crew. There is no guarantee they will accept me: a team living and working on its own out in the field is a tight little tribe, a family, and outsiders— Army, civilian, whatever they are—are not usually welcome.

I get Major Clark's Iraqi cell number from the 425th TOC and phone him. Luckily he remembers me from the walk-through of the bazaar, and has heard about my book project on the battalion grapevine. We arrange to meet the next time he and the team come out to BIAP; they will haul me and my gear back to Banzai with them, and we will play it by ear from there. "Hey, if I start driving you crazy, you can just tell me to leave," I reassure him.

"Oh, don't worry about that." Major Clark laughs. "If we don't like you, we'll throw you out in a second."

*   *   *

On May 27, Major Clark and his team show up at the A-LOC to pick up mail and some radio batteries from the supply room. They've told me they are coming, and I have my gear all packed. I jump in back of the second Humvee, along with my duffels, and we head back to Banzai.

It is a long, circuitous drive: first the deadly stretch of freeway known as Route Irish, where IEDs and ambushers kill Americans every week, straight to the Green Zone. Then in the main gate, next to the 14th of July Bridge, where there are regular suicide car bombings. Across the Green Zone, and out the Assassin's Gate, where signs remind us, HAIFA STREET IS CONDITION RED. Haifa would be the quickest route to Banzai, a straight-as-a-ruler shot north to al-Khadimiyah, but it is just too dangerous. Instead we wind around secondary streets till we hop up onto another freeway that passes a park and a ballet school, then miles of empty semi-wasteland, then a run-down industrial and car repair zone: comparatively safer, but the SAW-gunners are still watching every vehicle, every knot of pedestrians, every suspicious-looking bundle or trash pile by the roadside that might conceal a bomb.

Every moment along the way you never stop looking, staring: into dark courtyards (could be a shooter with an RPG in there), at rooftops (snipers), at the scores—hundreds—of vehicles around you in a traffic jam (suicide car bomber? mobile hit squad?). Every time you slow down on an on-ramp, pass an empty oil can, a fresh dirt pile or a fallen muffler (favorite IED loci), you find yourself flinching slightly, pulling your head back down into your body armor like a turtle, preparing yourself for

Sgt. Adam Grundman *(left)* and Maj. Mark Clark *(right)* planning missions
in the CAT-A 13 team-house office   *(Kimberly Frier)*

1st Sgt. Bob Paul *(left)* and interpreter al-Janabi *(right)* with wall map of al-Khadimiyah
in the team-house office   *(Rob Schultheis)*

Sgt. Paul and al-Janabi in the team-house office   *(Rob Schultheis)*

Sgt. Kramer and Spec. Kim "Beta" Frier working on one of the team's
balky Humvees in the team-house compound   *(Rob Schultheis)*

Maj. Clark *(left)* and Sgt. Grundman *(right)* on a mission in Old Bazaar   *(Rob Schultheis)*

Maj. Clark and Iraqi police checking out IED
near sewer pumping station in al-Hurriyah   *(Kimberly Frier)*

Maj. Clark and Spec. Jen "Espi" Espinosa overseeing a grain shipment
at the World Food Program food bank   *(Kimberly Frier)*

Spec. Espinosa and al-Khadimiyah schoolchildren. Iraqi kids were fascinated
by the team's two female soldiers, Espinosa and Frier   *(Kimberly Frier)*

Mosque Street and the al-Khadimiyah Shrine, burial place of two of the first four Shi'a Imams and one of the holiest pilgrimage sites for Shi'as around the world   *(Kimberly Frier)*

Crowds gathering in front of the shrine during the annual Ashura holy days; CAT-A 13 members and interpreter al-Janabi in foreground   *(Kimberly Frier)*

Sgt. Paul handing out toys to children *(Kimberly Frier)*

Spec. Frier with fans *(Kimberly Frier)*

Spec. Frier pulling security on rooftop across from al-Hurriyah DAC during evening
meeting of local Iraqi leaders and officers from the 1st Cavalry and Civil Affairs *(Kimberly Frier)*

Spec. Frier on SAW-gun during patrol in always-dangerous Taji. Note the up-armored Humvee,
which replaced the old open-backed "tubs" toward the end of CAT-A 13's stay in Iraq *(Kimberly Frier)*

Cpl. Cruddas, interpreter Ayat, Sgt. Paul, and Sgt. Grundman
in team-house compound   *(Kimberly Frier)*

Spec. Kramer receives Purple Heart, accompanied by Major Clark   *(Kimberly Frier)*

that sudden flash, boom, pinpoint of fire expanding to darkness that covers the world, a split second that you won't remember afterward that could leave you limbless, blind, castrated, eviscerated—a whole panoply of horrors that occur when gases expand at hypersonic speeds, bearing ax heads, daggers, razor blades of iron and steel shrapnel. . . .

After you've been in Baghdad awhile none of this really seems to bother you, it becomes as natural as commuting to work or driving to the beach on the weekend back in the States. You just *can't* be afraid of the place you live: it is not a matter of courage, but of biological necessity.

The consequences come later, when it is all over and you are back home: nightmares, eruptions of irrational rage, or simply long periods of time when your old life seems dull, empty, useless; you've gotten used to that keyed-up, intensified, adrenalized state, and the old beloved joys, friendships, pastimes don't seem special anymore. You find yourself almost longing for those Good Old Days among the killers.

Finally, as we approach the Tigris again, we exit the freeway into al-Khadimiyah, and drive north another couple of miles, past shade trees, houses, shops. Almost there.

Just short of Banzai, both Humvees pull up on the side of a traffic circle, next to a row of shops. It turns out the team wants to go grocery shopping. This may not sound remarkable, but it is: never in all my days out with the PHT and the Abu Ghraib CAT did we stop somewhere and do something like shop. I can already tell that life with CAT-A 13 is going to be very, very different.

Sergeant Paul has a grocery list, and while two troops stay on the Humvee SAW-guns, he leads everyone else from shop to shop, buying boxes of cake mix, sodas, shampoo, biscuits, cookies. Paul has evidently checked out the local cheeses before: he picks out two hard, ivory-colored varieties and a third that comes in satiny-soft snow-white blobs floating in a tub of cold water. All are really good, he assures me: "Better than the canned packaged shit from Europe." But his great love is the local bottled pomegranate juice he has discovered; he picks up two dozen bottles of the stuff.

Paul learned to forage for local foodstuffs years ago in Kenya, in the Peace Corps, where he dined on monkey, fried crickets, and live insect larvae the size of hot dogs, and after two months in Iraq he has an ever-growing list of favorites. The whole team seems right at home, joking with the merchants and trading small talk with Iraqi shoppers.

That evening, I begin to fit names to faces and faces to personalities. Major Clark has named his team "The Rogues," and it fits these wildly varied people.

Maj. Mark Clark: with his ruddy hatchet face, he looks like a cross between Chingachgook and Sheriff Sixgun out of a vintage Hollywood Western. Appropriate, because his hero is John Wayne; Clark regularly torments the rest of the team by watching DVDs of primitive black-and-white 1930s John Wayne serials for hours on the team's TV.

He is a character out of a time warp, a throwback to a more innocent era: at the age of forty-five he still gets phone calls from his father every week, making sure he is doing his duty the way he should. He imitates his father's gruff greeting affectionately: "HEY, BOY, HOW'RE YOU DOIN' OUT THERE?"

Clark is an ex–Green Beret, former member of the 10th Special Forces, the "Sneaky Petes." In the late seventies and early
eighties, at the height of the Cold War, the U.S. Armed Forces
were poised for a massive Soviet attack on Western Europe. As
the Red Army rolled through the Fulda Gap and out across West
Germany, Belgium, Holland and France, the 10th was to be airdropped deep behind enemy lines, in the outback of the USSR
itself. They would link up there with local insurgent groups and
conduct a guerrilla war and sabotage campaign until the war was
over.

After the Cold War fizzled out, Clark quit the Army and
went into the civilian business world; eventually he ended up
running the global teleconferencing system for Bank of America.
When the Iraq War began, he was living in the Bay Area with a
wife and two young daughters, periodically jetting around the
world for international banking conferences. Now, less than a
year later, he has quit his job, his wife has left him, and he is back
in uniform in Iraq running a team of Army Civil Affairs reservists; and he is happy, totally in his element. He tells me that
when he was a boy growing up in Germany—his father was a
GI—his parents took him to Dachau, and he saw an old Jewish
man weeping over the lists of the people who died there. "I decided right then I hated bullies, people who hurt innocent people," he tells me. "That's why I joined SF, and that's why I came
to Iraq." From anyone else these words would seem false,
phony, but they ring true coming from the Major.

Sgt. Bob Paul is round-faced, hard-eyed, head shaved bald;
he looks like the meanest guy at an Iggy Pop/Stooges revival.

Another forty-something soldier, "Sarnt Paul" was a Peace Corps volunteer in Kenya for three years, went on to work at Peace Corps HQ in Washington after that, and was an urban planner in The Dalles, Oregon, when his reserve battalion, the 425th, was called up for Iraq. Like Major Clark, he left a wrecked marriage back in the States; his wife took off for Texas with their daughter shortly before he left. He has a brilliant mind and lacerating wit, combined with a classic hard-core sergeant's attitude. His favorite pastime at home: high-risk whitewater kayaking.

Sergeant Lawrence, aka "Fat Larry," isn't fat at all but he is "Fat Larry" forever anyway; Sergeant Paul even uses the sobriquet over the radio: "Fat Larry. Come in, Fat Larry. Fat Larry, acknowledge." An accountant back home in the Midwest, he is excited about being in Iraq, and he tells me his dream is to be a kind of mercenary adventurer, wandering the world, having adventures, doing "cool things" and meeting "awesome women." He seems to have no problem with the latter: every few days he gets a letter or a parcel from a different "girlfriend" back home. So Fat Larry is a ladies' man: go figure.

KRAMER, in caps, is slight, sinewy, flint-eyed, red-faced, with a saurian smile. He killed two Iraqis as a Marine sniper in the Gulf War—fired a TOW missile into their tank—and two American "motherfuckers" when he was a policeman in California: "Hell, when I was a cop, motherfuckers shot me four times and stabbed me five." In addition to the bullet and knife wounds, he has by his own account crashed his Harley over a guardrail at a hundred miles an hour, had a Chevy sedan fall on him when a jack slipped, and been dragged a hundred yards by a drunk woman motorist he had pulled over, who stomped on the gas while he was leaning in her car window. "I 'bout beat her to death when she finally stopped," he says cheerfully.

In addition to his police career he has been at one time or another a master chef, carpenter, plumber, electrician, mechanic and heavy equipment operator. He now lives in rural Missouri with his wife and two kids, working as a butcher. He spends hours every night talking to her online.

As I will find out, there's a whole lot more to Kramer than first meets the eye.

Adam Grundman is a stocky, muscle-bound clean-cut Iowan, another Midwestern reservist yanked to reinforce the 425th; he is in his mid-thirties but looks ten years younger. Has a liberal arts degree with an English lit major from Northern Iowa; after graduation he spent four or five years in the Seabees. When he gets home from Iraq, he will marry his college sweetheart and go to work in his dad's small town insurance firm. But beneath this *It's a Wonderful Life* façade is a brilliant, brooding mercurial soul, who dreams of being a standup comic in New York and without warning goes into impromptu comedy routines, like the one where he alternates between being a hyperenthusiastic Borscht Belt comic on tour in Iraq and the stony-faced uncomprehending audience: "Anybody here from Mosul?"—a blankly staring face—"Hey, how about that al-Sadr guy? Is he a crazy character, or what?"— the blank face again—"Good night, everybody! You've been a great audience! BE SURE AND TRY THE VEAL!"

* * *

Shane Cruddas is a big heavyset Hispanic kid, recently married, with a new baby back home in L.A. The second night I am with the team we celebrate his twenty-first birthday: Kramer takes it upon himself to bake a cake and make hamburgers, pasta and deviled eggs. Espinosa buys another cake at one of Banzai's hajji shops and everybody sings "Happy Birthday." Afterward, Cruddas borrows the Major's cell phone, goes out into the garden and calls his wife. When he returns you can see the homesickness in his eyes: happy twenty-first in the middle of a war zone, twelve thousand miles from his loved ones.

Product of a broken home in Washington, D.C., Cruddas grew up tough, running the streets with a local gang and in and out of trouble till his stepmother finally threw him out. He moved to southern California and rejoined his mom's family, settled down and was working his way up as a Terminix exterminator in the Valley when without warning his country called. He shows me his collection of family photos: "This is my kid sister and her boyfriend—I told him if he ever touched her I'd kill him. This is my cousin Rudy—on weekends we road race cars together on the freeway. Here I am at my mom's folks' big reunion last year—my face is all fucked up because some Latin Bloods jumped me on my way there."

Cruddas's virtual religion is rebuilding hot Japanese compacts, but when he tries to tell me about it he may as well be speaking Martian: "I put a four-barrel Hinson carb on it with a Wakahashi air scoop, then I added a tuned Gabrielli exhaust manifold," and so on. All too many of his car stories end the same way: "I had it two weeks when I wrapped it up doing 128 miles an hour on the 5."

I've been with the team less than a week when he gives me the name I will be known by the rest of my time with them: "Writer Rob. Because your name is Rob, and you're a writer." He beams, hugely pleased with himself for thinking of it. Heart of gold.

Jen Espinosa, aka "Espi," is a pretty freckle-faced brunette heartbreaker. She was working part-time as a cocktail waitress in Socal, surfing the beaches around Laguna and studying Mandarin at the Army Language School in Monterey when the 425th was called up for Iraq. (Espi is telling us about waitressing at a popular bar at Universal City when the irrepressible Cruddas chimes in, "Hey, I know that place! My homeys and I got in a big-ass fight with some other guys in the parking lot there one night.") Most likely Espi could have gotten out of going to Iraq—she was at or near the top of her class at Monterey—but she felt "like I should go, 'cause everybody else in the battalion was." A natural linguist, she has already picked up a fair amount of Iraqi street Arabic and has taught herself enough of the Arab alphabet to make out street signs.

Sgt. Lynn Goff is young, awkward and overweight, with crew-cut red hair and glasses. She seems out of place in Iraq, in the Army and on the team: too immature and unsure of herself for her rank, she tries to make up for it by barking out orders and talking tough, which only makes people more determined to ignore her.

* * *

Al-Janabi and Ajay: the team roll would not be complete without the two Shi'a interpreters. Al-Janabi is a distinguished-looking gray-haired gentleman, always impeccably dressed, who was educated in England. An ex–airline pilot and former Iraqi Air Force general, he isn't shy about his opinion of his homeland: "It is finished, and there is nothing here for me." Despite his cosmopolitan mien, he is very serious about his faith, and will happily discuss the fine points of Shi'a theology, jurisprudence and history with anyone who is interested, which basically means me.

The rotund Ajay, on the other hand, is your typical twenty-first-century big-city kid, similar to the PHT's interpreter Ron in that you could plonk him down in L.A., London, New York or Prague and he would fit right in. While al-Janabi is discussing Iraqi politics with Major Clark or explaining the esoterica of the *Najulbagha* of Hazrat Ali to me, Ajay is reminiscing fondly about holidays on the nude beaches of Turkey, channel-surfing the TV in the team room for soft porn channels, or complaining about how unhip (i.e., "moral") his Iraqi girlfriends are.

I begin sussing out my new home.

The FOB where CAT-A 13 is based was originally called Dakota: Col. Miles Miyamasu, who commands the 1st Battalion of the 5th Regiment of the 1st Cavalry Division, renamed the base Banzai to honor his third-generation Japanese-American roots. This same sense of esprit also applies to the 1/5 Cav, traditionally known as the "Black Knights": a sign on the south gate reads BANZAI PATROL BASE, HOME OF THE BLACK KNIGHTS, and the battalion TOC, housed in an old Iraqi Army office block in the center of the post, boasts a two-story-high sign bearing the stylized image of a knight charging on horseback. Next to the TOC, other former Iraqi Army buildings house the DFAC (mess hall) and a gym. West of the TOC area is the landmark known as "Smiley-Face Saddam": formerly a portrait of the Iraqi dictator elevated on a concrete pillar, it has been repainted with the classic round yellow cartoon visage made famous on stickers and T-shirts, so that Mr. Smiley is wearing Saddam's trademark beret. "Some kind of funny shit," Cruddas says of it, and he is right.

Banzai occupies a big area, approximately two miles by two miles, bounded on the east by the Tigris River, and on the other three sides by the neighborhood of al-Khadimiyah. From the north gate of Banzai you can see the ethereal golden dome and minarets of the al-Khadimiyah shrine, where the second and fourth Shi'a imams are buried. The south gate is right next to the river and beneath one of the main bridges connecting east and west Baghdad; almost every night Bad Guys from Sadr City or the hardcore Sunni Adhamiyah district sneak out onto the bridge and shoot at the gate guards with AK-47s and RPGs.

Banzai consists of a palm tree–studded expanse of warehouses, parking lots, Quonset huts, barracks and scattered single-storey structures, some bombed out during the assault on Baghdad, many occupied by the Cav. Two big five-story brick buildings behind the CAT-A 13 compound house most of the Cav troops; the buildings look like college dorms back in the United States, except the parking lots surrounding them are crowded with Abrams tanks, Bradley fighting vehicles, M-113s and Humvees instead of Saabs, Vanagons and SUVs.

Across the street from our compound's gate is a swimming pool complex where Republican Guard officers once splashed and cavorted; it is usually closed for one reason or another. The view that way, with its swaying palm trees and cabana-like buildings, looks surreally like a shabby beach resort in Thailand or Mexico; the illusion vanishes when you look past it and see the wide, sluggish waters of the Tigris, and beyond that the domes, villas and housing blocks of east Baghdad, where more often than not smoke is rising—from the latest air strike, terrorist bombing or street fighting.

Iraqi National Guard recruits, young men and women who have signed up to try to defend the new post-Saddam Iraq, live and train in the far southwest corner of the base, and there are two or three mysterious off-limits areas housing SF Secret Squirrels and shadowy characters in civilian garb. There are hajji shops here and there; the one closest to the CAT-A 13 compound is called the Moonlight Café, and when the team is off-duty there are usually two or three members over there, e-mailing or calling home.

The CAT-A 13 compound is in the northeast corner of Banzai: a walled quarter acre of palm trees and scrubby gardens adorned by an elaborate fountain with leaping concrete dolphins and a wishing well; both fountain and well are bone dry. In the rear is a ramshackle air raid shelter. The compound is centered around two single-story stucco buildings that once were homes and offices for Iraqi Military Intelligence officers. The main building houses the team's office, living quarters, a bathroom, storeroom and TV room. Major Clark lives in the second building, in an austere chamber strewn with maps, tools, books and a mattress on the floor for sleeping; I end up moving in with him, dragging in an Army cot and setting it up against one wall. The rest of the building is taken up by what was once a sauna room and is now a shower. Both buildings are air-conditioned, when the electricity doesn't fail.

Between the driveway and the two buildings is a tin-roofed area where the team has set up a makeshift kitchen and a table and chairs where people sit, smoke and talk. There is an Iraqi-style toilet behind a thin metal door that does little to contain the fetid odors that rise from the hole in the floor. On the side of the main house an unsteady steel ladder leads up to a flat roof, crudely fortified with clumps of sandbags and bricks here and there. There is another toilet, a plastic portable outhouse, just outside the gate. It's a pretty nice hooch, for Baghdad in 2004.

A good team is more than a sum of its parts, and it doesn't happen by accident. My second or third evening at Banzai, Major Clark explains to me how he put CAT-A 13 together back at Fort Bragg.

They were housed in the old barracks at Bragg, the ones with long rooms packed with bunk beds in endless rows. "Different CA teams were bunched together with no space to hang out and talk and give members of the same team the chance to get to know each other," Major Clark recalls. "Right away I saw this wasn't going to work if I wanted to really put my team together before we headed for Iraq: it's nearly impossible to organize things or have team meetings when you're always having people walk by, with the sound of hundreds of soldiers talking, laughing, banging around so loud you can't carry on a conversation."

Inevitably, the Major came up with a solution: "First I measured how much space our four sets of bunks took up, and then we rearranged our team's bunks so they made a square, one bunk on each side facing in, forming an enclosed area between them that was all ours. I even made the square eighteen inches less than the original space they allotted us; I knew how much those old sergeant majors who run the barracks at Bragg hate any kind of change from the official routine, and I wasn't about to give them an excuse for coming down on us."

Just as the Major had predicted, "The new arrangement worked even better than I thought it would; everyone on the team really liked having a space that was just for us, where they could get together and talk and joke around, or just escape the crowds and the noise and read, write letters or whatever. Pretty soon people from other teams were dropping by to visit, and other team leaders started talking about rearranging their bunks the same way.

"Of course, when that happened, the sergeant major in charge of our barracks building went crazy: for something like twenty years he had had 'his' barracks laid out exactly according to the regulations, right down to the last half inch, and now it was all changing. To him it was like a mutiny, an act of treason. He wrote up an emergency order, telling us to move our bunks back the way they were or he would issue me an Article 15 and remove me from command, break up the team, bust everyone else a pay grade.

"Some of our people started laughing at him, which made things worse. I couldn't blame them: here we were, going off to war, and I know for a fact this guy had never been deployed outside the U.S. during a whole lifetime in the Army, and he was screaming at us about how important it was to stick to the system even if we didn't understand why. He actually stood there and watched while we moved all our gear out of the way and dragged our bunks around till they were lined up with all the others again. But we had already had a real chance to get it together during the week and a half when we had our space, and the funny thing was, when the sergeant major came down on us, it just pulled the team together even more."

Major Clark shows the same ingenuity handling the team as he did assembling it. He likes to talk to his soldiers one on one, whether he is correcting some past mistake or getting their input on a new idea. He will come into the room where everyone is sitting, pick someone out and say, "Let's go take a walk." The pair of them will walk around the yard, out of earshot of the rest of the team, for anywhere from five minutes to an hour, however long it takes to work things out. He also likes to enliven premission briefings with what he calls "So what?" questions, though a better name might be "What then?" "What if we see a bunch of broken windows or doors that need replacing?" he asks, when we are about to visit the school in Dafur where we are building a kitchen for the teachers and staff. "Are we going to just forget it, or should we think about starting another project to get it fixed?" Or, "What if the people at the al-Shula DAC don't want to talk to us? They may be worried they'll become targets if they're seen meeting with Americans, or maybe they just look at us as enemies. Start thinking about it, because if we don't work with the DAC, how're we going to work there?" "What do we do if people in a crowd start throwing stones at us, and we're boxed in so we can't move the vehicles?"

"A rock can kill you," Fat Larry says.

"That's exactly my point. Rocks *can* kill you, but what do you do about it?"

"Shoot the motherfuckers," Kramer growls, but he doesn't really mean it. He's a Marine, and Marines follow orders; and if the Rules of Engagement say you can't shoot people for throwing stones at you, then he'll sit behind his SAW-gun and take it till he's dead.

"So what do we do?" Grundman asks.

"I don't know the answer," the Major says. "That's why I'm asking. I want all of you to keep asking those kinds of questions." Socrates with an M-16.

It's this kind of leadership that keeps CAT-A 13 safe; Major Clark never lets the team slide into what I think of as "sleep-soldiering": going through the motions, drifting through routines with minds on autopilot and senses in neutral. That's how you end up doing a half-assed job, and get killed doing it.

Most important is Major Clark's docrine of Fitting In. "I've told everyone on the team to think of al-Khadimiyah as if it's our neighborhood too, and to always act like we belong here," he says. "We don't act like we're always uncomfortable and afraid, like we're strangers, out of our depth and unsure of ourselves. On the other hand, we don't swagger around like we run the place: after all, this is Iraq, and it belongs to the Iraqis in the end. The people here are our neighbors, and we are theirs. The more we fit into al-Khadimiyah, the better we're doing our job." At one point Major Clark tries to get permission to fly the new Iraqi national flag from our vehicles; the Big Army smacks the idea down, but he never stops thinking that it was a great idea.

7

I HAVE JOINED the team at a dodgy time. During the recent Ashura, the annual Shi'a holy days commemorating the martyrdom of the religion's founder Ali, al-Qaeda terrorists attacked the al-Khadimiyah shrine. Hundreds of pilgrims were killed or injured by bombs and RPG rounds fired from rooftops. In the aftermath of the slaughter, mobs raged through the streets outside Banzai, protesting the United States' failure to protect Iraqi Shi'ites; almost daily Shi'a mosques are being destroyed by car bombs and Shi'a worshippers gunned down. When armored Humvees manned by military police showed up to monitor the situation, demonstrators stoned them; one SAW-gunner was hit in the head, but to their credit the soldiers kept their cool and held their fire.

Thanks in a large part to those American troops' courage, the neighborhood returned to relative normalcy, and now the religious scholars and mullahs from the shrine have a kind of hot line set up to the Cav TOC at Banzai: when troublemakers show up from outside, or street rumors spread about attacks on U.S. troops, the Shi'a elders call up the Cav and help plan how to deal with it. Often the people of al-Khadimiyah take care of things themselves: after the Ashura bombings, several spurious "Shi'a pilgrims" from outside Iraq, reportedly found with weapons, explosives or shaky bona fides, were quietly done away with by the locals.

The Army in the person of the 1/5 Cav has a special relationship with the al-Khadimiyah Shi'as, thanks to Colonel Miyamasu and his savvy staff officers. The street leading from Banzai to the shrine is guarded by local religious militiamen, serious-looking young men in dark clothing, armed with AK-47s, under an agreement between the Cav and the elders from the mosque.

Before Ashura, soldiers from Banzai were actually welcome to visit the shrine—Iranian Shi'as who came to Baghdad to visit this holiest of holy spots used to clamor to have their photographs taken with GIs—but now by unwritten agreement troops don't go there unless specially invited. (The Iranian pilgrims are gone, too; the corrupt mullahs in Tehran were none too happy to see their countrymen visiting Iraq, the authentic birthplace of Shi'ism.)

Major Clark has done his part by proposing a memorial to the pilgrims slain during Ashura, to be built on the circular park in the center of the intersection leading to the shrine; it will be inscribed with the names of the more than two hundred men, women and children killed in the bombings. The mullahs from the shrine have approved the project, and several Iraqi architects and designers, all Shi'as of course, are submitting designs for the memorial.

But al-Khadimiyah is a huge area, covering most of northwestern Baghdad, and not all of it is as peaceful as the area around the shrine. On the northern edge of the city is the slum neighborhood called al-Shula, populated by a mix of Shi'as and

Sunnis, and it is pretty much Bandit Country. A few days before
I joined the team, they were checking out a broken sewer line
there when a large crowd gathered. The team's interpreters, Ajay
and al-Janabi, overheard a group of men talking conspiratorially
of delaying the soldiers long enough to get enough reinforcements to overwhelm them: "We'll kill them all, and burn their
vehicles." The two interpreters interrupted the plotters, calling
them bad Moslems for wanting to murder people who had come
to try to help them. As the crowd joined in, some agreeing with
the conspirators and other taking the side of the Americans, the
interpreters and the CAT-A 13 crew Irened the area.

North and east of al-Shula is another dodgy area, Taji. An
incongruous mosaic of city and farmland, it includes pockets of
pro-Saddam peasants reinforced by hard-core resistance fighters
from the Sunni Triangle to the west. The tiny American firebase
there is mortared and rocketed almost every night, and several
soldiers have been killed or wounded. The place is so hazardous
that reinforcements and supplies often helicopter in under cover
of night. Much of Taji is also in the team's AO, and they will be
working there a lot.

But no place here is immune to danger. Just before I joined
the team, the CAT-A 13 troops were checking out a warehouse
in the abandoned industrial zone in central al-Khadimiyah; before the war this was a busy manufacturing center employing
thousands of workers, but it is all shut down now thanks to the
U.S. bombing campaign, looting and the overall breakdown of
the Iraqi economy. The contents of this particular warehouse
turned out to be disturbing, to say the least: hundreds of tons of
chlorine in cylinders with Iraqi Air Force markings, along with
similar amounts of chemicals used to generate chlorine gas.

Chlorine has perfectly innocent uses, of course—Baghdad's water purification plants rely on it, just as similar treatment facilities in the West do—but the military markings and the warehouse's location in a mostly Shi'a civilian neighborhood suggest the cache may have had a much more sinister purpose, as a kind of Doomsday Device to be used if Baghdad's Shi'as rose up against Saddam Hussein's regime. There is more than enough chlorine here to kill every Shi'a man, woman and child in Sadr City and al-Khadimiyah.

Now, with Saddam gone, the stash is a tailor-made WMD for terrorists to use against our troops. All you would have to do is haul a couple of truckloads upwind of BIAP and Camp Victory and loose the stuff into the atmosphere: you could kill thirty or forty thousand American soldiers in a single night. Whoever owns the warehouse has posted a couple of rent-a-guards here, but they wouldn't even try to stop a group of hard-core al-Qaeda jihadis. In fact, the security guards told Major Clark that a "man from Lebanon" showed up just a couple of weeks ago, gave them a receipt and hauled away a whole semi-load of the stuff.

Major Clark immediately informed Colonel Miyamasu of the deadly find, and together they kicked a high-priority message up the line to brigade, requesting immediate action to safeguard the site, or relocate the chemicals in a more secure location: even if terrorists don't get to steal some of the stuff and use it, a stray mortar round or rocket could hit the warehouse and accidentally trigger a catastrophic release of gas that would kill thousands of Iraqi civilians and hundreds of U.S. soldiers stationed at Banzai. The brass's response was "Really, really sorry, there's nothing we can do: we can't spare enough troops to guard the warehouse, and as far as moving the chemicals is concerned the problem is the same, not enough manpower and vehicles to safely transport them out of Baghdad, and no safe place to put them anyway." It is the same old story here as it is all across Iraq: not enough boots on too much ground.

I soon discover that the members of CAT-A 13 are hard to faze; they possess the kind of blasé insouciance usually associated with foppish fictional British heroes like James Bond or the Scarlet Pimpernel, who act like danger is just too tedious to dwell on: their sangfroid borders on the hilarious. My third day out with the team we have our nearly disastrous encounter with the Sadr Brigades in east Baghdad. When Major Clark asks the team members to go over the day's events in the evening afteraction review, they want to talk about everything but the mob scene.

It turns out that Sergeant Paul, who is an indefatigable shopper, was also checking out east Baghdad's shops and bazaars during the mission. When Major Clark asks for input about the mission, Paul comes out with something totally unexpected.

"Did anyone else see those parrots?" he asks.

Everyone looks at him with a baffled expression.

"I saw this amazing pet store while we were looking for the orphanage," he continues. "I'm not kidding, the guy must have had a hundred different kinds of birds in cages out front. There were a couple of beautiful parrots, huge ones—I've never seen anything like them; they must have been a foot high, with blue, red and yellow tail feathers. If we ever go back there, I'm going to buy one."

The ever-enthusiastic Cruddas is instantly inspired.

"Do you think they'd let you take it back to the States?" he asks Sergeant Paul. "It would be so fucking cool, to have an Iraqi parrot for a souvenir!"

Kramer utters a curt, disparaging laugh. "Cruddas, if you buy a motherfucking raghead parrot, I'll kill it, cook it and make it into tacos, and then I'll make you eat the whole goddamned thing."

"Aww, you don't mean that," Cruddas says.

"Why don't you try me?" He doesn't really mean it: he and Cruddas are actually the best of buddies, Kramer like a big bad brother and Cruddas his sidekick and biggest fan.

Fat Larry chimes in: "I didn't see any parrots, but they had awesome-looking pomegranates at this one market, piles of them."

Instantly Sergeant Paul turns on him. "You should've told me! I would have made the Major pull over so we could buy some." Paul is always scouting for new foods, and among his discoveries is locally bottled pomegranate juice, but up till now he hasn't found any of the actual fruit.

Major Clark sits there listening to his team with a faint, quizzical smile, as if he can't quite believe his ears.

Meanwhile Kramer and Cruddas have segued inevitably into their ritual one-upmanship routine, Hispanic versus Redneck. "You people in Missouri hate everybody, don't you, Kramer?" Cruddas says mischievously. "I'll bet you belong to the Ku Klux Klan."

"The Klan? Yeah, we've got some of them in Missouri." Kramer looks back at Cruddas, his smile widening at the edges till his back teeth gleam. "I hate them, too—motherfuckers in their stupid fucking white sheets burning crosses. I'll bet if I went out some night with my AK-47 and sent a few rounds their way they'd get rid of those *white sheets* pretty fast."

"I can't believe you didn't tell me about those pomegranates," Sergeant Paul says to Fat Larry, shaking his head. "What good are you, anyway?"

Grundman is oblivious to all the chatter: he just got a package of books mailed from home, and he is buried in the opening pages of *The Odyssey*. Grundman was an English lit major at Northern Iowa, and he adores myths, from Homer and Virgil to the superheroes in Marvel comics. Periodically he gets off the Internet and reports excitedly on the latest arcane comic heroes to make it onto the movie screen: "Hey, they're making *Mongoose Man and Gorilla Girl* into a movie! Adam Sandler's going to play Mongoose Man, and that Canadian model, the one who was in *Species*, with the a-*ma*-zing bod—"

"Natasha Henstridge?"

"Natasha Henstridge, that's right, she's gonna be Gorilla Girl—"

"She was the one who killed guys with her hooters in that British movie, what was it? *Death Ray*," Fat Larry interjects.

"No way," Grundman says scornfully. "And they've got Donald Sutherland as Professor Pandora, he'll be perfect, and some kid I've never heard of as Billy. Man, I hope we're back home when it comes out, I don't want to see it two months later in some crappy little octoplex without Sensurround—"

Espinosa is on one of the computers in the office, headphones on her ears, the faint echo of a No Doubt song leaking out, adding up the budget for one of her projects: she is in charge of beautifying two of al-Khadimiyah's main traffic circles, turning dead grass and dust into pocket parks with flower beds and benches, places for local residents to hang out in the evening. It may not seem like important work, in a city ravaged by violence and unemployment, but Major Clark has a theory about this, too; he seems to have a theory about nearly everything. When the Washington, D.C., Metro system was built, the stations and trains were designed to be immune to dirt, trash and graffiti, and since then, studies have shown that the clean, orderly environment has had far less crime than other, funkier urban rail systems.

If you make a place *look* normal, it encourages the return of normal life; if people feel like they can get away with ignoring the little rules, they'll end up breaking the big important ones, too. Squalor = anarchy.

Later, I join Major Clark outside as a couple of mortar rounds go off, over toward the south gate of Banzai; the usual 60mm, fired from across the river in Adhamiyah. The 1st Armored Division guys over there, they call their FOB "Gunner Palace," have their hands full. The locals are hard-core Sunnis, and the big mosque there is Wahabi Central: when the neighborhood *shebab* aren't shooting at the AD or trying to blow them up with IEDs, they like to lob mortar shells into Banzai, and they do it *all the damned time,* day and night.

We listen for a while, and then I ask the Major if he is going to continue trying to free the wrongly accused Iraqi security guards. We are in the midst of a war-torn country that is in imminent danger of falling into anarchy and taking the whole Middle East with it, along with America's status as the world's only superpower. Can the team really take the time to try to save two unlucky Iraqis?

Major Clark gives me a classic John Wayne look. "Well, if I got put in jail for something I didn't do, I'd want someone to help me," he says. "Wouldn't you?"

There is a list on the wall of the team house office, of the missions CAT-A 13 is currently involved in, and the budget for each. Some of the typical ones are

> MANHOLE COVERS—$46.5K
> AL-KHADIMIYAH DISTRICT COUNCIL—$10K
> MAINTENANCE YARD—$9050
> HURRIYAH NEIGHBORHOOD SEWER REPAIRS—$33K
> HURRIYAH SEWER SUBSTATION UPGRADES—$49K

Each and every project goes through a process whose rules are also posted in the team house office:

1. IDENTIFY A PROJECT THAT REQUIRES A REQUEST FOR BIDS.
2. REQUESTS FOR BIDS ARE WRITTEN BY US AND TRANSLATED BY ONE OF OUR INTERPRETERS. THESE ARE POSTED AT THE DAC.
3. THE BIDS ARE RECEIVED AT THE DAC AND WE WILL PICK THESE UP PERIODICALLY.
4. THE SOLDIER RESPONSIBLE FOR THE PROJECT MAKES A RECOMMENDATION FOR WHO GETS THE BID AWARD.
5. COMPLETE THE "PRB" AND ATTACH THE RECOMMENDED CONTRACTOR BID. (SEE GRUNDMAN) IF THE PROJECT EXCEEDS 10K. ATTACH ALL THE OTHER BIDS, AND THERE MUST BE A TOTAL OF AT LEAST THREE BIDS. A PICTURE MUST BE

SUBMITTED WITH EACH BID WHICH WILL CONSTITUTE THE "BEFORE" PICTURE AS A POWERPOINT SLIDE.

6. THREE PICTURES ARE REQUIRED. A BEFORE, DURING AND AFTER PHOTOGRAPH. THESE MUST BE TAKEN FROM THE SAME VANTAGE POINT. NO SOLDIERS IN THE PHOTO.

7. AFTER THE BID IS SUCCESSFULLY AWARDED, THE CONTRACTOR WILL BE PAID ON A THURSDAY AT THE DAC. IT IS THE SOLDIER'S RESPONSIBILITY TO ENSURE CONTACT IS MADE AND THE CONTRACTOR ARRIVES. THE SECOND PICTURE IS DUE AT THE SECOND PAYMENT WITH THE UPDATED POWERPOINT SLIDE.

The system puts each team member in charge of one or more aid project—Clark tries to match Cruddas with santitation improvements, where his experience as an exterminator will be useful; the ex-city planner Sergeant Paul with traffic and civil administration; and so on. It also means that the team handles a huge amount of money, especially by Iraqi standards: the cash is stashed in a big iron safe in the office, and every contract payment is painstakingly recorded and rerecorded in a series of forms.

One day, as we drive back to Banzai from the DAC compound, we come upon a crowd of young men shouting angrily and raising fists in the air. The Major immediately has us pull over and stop, and before the lead Humvee has stopped rolling he's out the door and striding into the middle of the mob. Sergeant Paul and Cruddas start to jump out to guard him, but he motions them back. We watch him listen to the men, shake his head and reply in his rudimentary Arabic. Those closest to him turn to their friends in the rear and explain what the Major is saying. Smiles begin to appear on faces. As Major Clark returns to the convoy, he turns to wave and calls out, "*Ma'asalaama.*" The crowd actually cheers as we drive away and, looking back, we see them dispersing.

"What was that all about?" I ask him when we arrive back at the compound.

"Somebody at CPA announced we were recruiting for a new course for police recruits, but when these guys showed up today there was no course, no recruiters, nothing. Somebody called and checked, and the CPA told them they'd given out the wrong date, the course started a week ago and there weren't going to be any more."

He goes on into the office, and thirty seconds later he is on the phone to CPA. I overhear, "Well, if you aren't responsible, let me talk to someone who is." "No, right now." "Well then, find him . . ." Tenacious as a pit bull or The Duke, he's on the phone for over thirty minutes before he hangs up. He sighs and looks over at me. "They say they're going to accept another class of recruits later this month, and they'll let me know as soon as they set the dates."

"That's great."

"Yeah, if you believe them. I don't." He picks up the phone again. "I'm going to call Colonel Miyamasu and have him kick it up to the division. CPA doesn't care if some lowly major complains, but if Colonel Formica calls them they'll jump." He starts dialing. "I don't know how we expect the Iraqis to help us when they try to and we slam the door in their face." That's extremely strong talk, coming from the ever-loyal and soft-spoken Major, and I can tell he is raging inside.

That evening we are outside taking in the usual

entertainment—distant explosions, a burst of gunfire over by the main gate, a flash and an arc of tracer fire across the river—when Major Clark turns to me and says, "You know, one of these days I'm going to walk out into one of those crowds, and somebody's going to shoot me in the head." He doesn't seem particularly excited or upset about it; he is just stating the obvious, that CAT-A 13 is pushing the odds, operating out on the edge the way they do, and someday their luck is going to run out.

Another day the team is way up north in Tajji, where the city gives way to palm groves, green fields and ancient villages. The farmers up there have complained about the big American firing range to the northeast: it seems that when the ordnance engineers detonate multi-ton piles of old munitions, the explosions are cracking walls and breaking windows in the villages. Since Taji is in our AO, the Major decided to go up there and see what was up, even though the area the team headed to was prime insurgent turf.

There's a definite feel of punching the envelope, pushing luck, as we leave the main road and follow the GPS coordinates down a narrow dirt lane through tunnel-like vegetation. If someone wanted to potshot or ambush our two open Humvees, we would be lunch. But when the vehicles finally emerge into the plaza of the village, people come pouring out of houses, waving and smiling. It looks like they are somehow expecting the team. Someone dashes off to get the mayor; he appears a couple of minutes later, a tubby glad-handing character in spotless white tribal robes accompanied by a retinue of retainers. Al-Janabi, the Major and Sergeant Paul meet them in the middle of the plaza, and they discuss the problem of the explosions from the firing range.

The Major tells the mayor he is sorry about the whole situation, that the explosions aren't going to stop, it's part of a Big Picture beyond the understanding or control of humble souls like majors and mayors, but that the villagers can go to the firing range with their damage claims and get paid reparations in cash; the Army engineers have already given the okay. The villagers seem overjoyed at the news. Kramer, surveying the scene from behind his SAW-gun, offers his inevitable sour commentary: "Hah! Motherfuckers'll find a crack in some fucked-up two-cent wall their grandfather built and go collect ten thousand dollars."

"Hey, we're supposed to be helping rebuild their economy, aren't we?" I say brightly, just to provoke the irascible ex-Marine.

He gives me a look both scathing and amused—he knows exactly what I'm up to, and barks a terminal condemnation of "this motherfucking worthless raghead country." A moment later he is smiling benignly at a tiny Iraqi child who is gazing up at him with enormous admiring eyes, and when he thinks no one is looking he gives his little fan a wave.

You would think the mission here would be over, but with Major Clark you never know. Before we leave, he consults the map and spots another village a couple of miles farther on. When he asks the mayor about the place, the villagers begin shouting: "Those people are no good—they hate Americans and they love Saddam—if you go there they will kill you!" If the Major had any doubts, that clinches it. Looking like a man who just won the lottery, he turns to us: "Change of mission. I want to check out that next village."

On the way back to the Humvees, I see Sergeant Paul stop the Major and talk to him quietly: "We're supposed to be at the DAC in a little over an hour, sir."

"Don't worry, we'll make it," the Major says confidently. Sergeant Paul raises his eyes heavenward as they re-ass the Humvees, and a moment later we're roaring out of the village, deeper into the terra incognita of palm jungle and jade-green brush.

The first thing we see when we reach the next village is a wall plastered with Saddam Hussein and Ba'ath Party posters. But before anyone can tell the Major "I told you so," diminutive Iraqis are popping up everywhere around us, exulting and calling out honorific greetings. These people look different from the other Iraqis we have seen in Taji: they are small, slim, their faces sharper and finer than the big Babylonian features of so many Baghdadites, and the women are dressed in rainbows of fiery primary colors.

They are Marsh Arabs, refugees from the ancient water-world of the Tigris-Euphrates delta far to the south. Two decades ago Saddam Hussein built a massive network of dykes and canals and drained the delta, destroying the vast marshlands, estuaries, lagoons and archipelagos and uprooting the Marsh Arabs who had lived there for millennia: these unique, little-known people were Shi'as, automatically branding them as enemies in Saddam's eyes, and their remote dwellings on uncharted islets and floating meadows of reeds placed them outside the Baghdad government's control. Hundreds of square miles of rich fisheries and avian migration sanctuaries were reduced to barren mudflats; emerald islands turned into clumps of tinder-dry deadfall. The Iraqi Army torched tens of thousands of acres of twenty-foot-tall papyrus reeds and rushes; for months the skies over southern Iraq were black with smoke.

Over the centuries the Marsh Arabs had adapted to their secret paradise with marvelous ingenuity. Nineteen fifties photographs by Wilfred Thesiger and Gavin Maxwell, two of the only outsiders to visit this Lost World before Saddam destroyed it, show hand-carved longboats with upcurved prows as sharp as arrows, woven-reed guesthouses the size of Quonset huts and as airy and graceful as Japanese paper lanterns, floating papyrus hunting blinds camouflaged with clumps of brush, and water buffalos grazing on artificial islands no larger than a motel room. Safe in this trackless territory, the Marsh Arabs huffed their homegrown ganja and sang songs celebrating their private internecine feuds and wars:

> "He does not want a buffalo
> He does not want a hundred sheep
> But his rifle and dagger are deadly."

They also battled the gargantuan savage wild boars that were their deadliest enemies, as described by Gavin Maxwell, who visited them in the 1950s with famed explorer Wilfred Thesiger: "wounds [from boar attacks] are often fatal . . . and many of the [Marsh Arabs] carry scars of past gorings. . . . Pigs will even attack a large canoe, and Thesiger told me he has seen the bow of a 36 foot tarada stove in this way."

This splendid age-old way of life died along with the delta in a few short years, and the Marsh Arabs fled north into the hellish deserts and cities of Iraq: from Lords of their World to starving, homeless vagabonds in a blink of history's eye. Now they are camped out across Iraq, wherever they can find an abandoned village or an empty urban wasteland; the team will later find a whole community of them surviving in a toxic waste dump in southern Taji, surrounded by ponds of poison water: a hideous twenty-first-century parody of the old delta. CA work is hard on the soul: it means viewing the world at its very worst, from the long-suffering bottom up—the injustice, injured innocence and sorrow of it all.

The Saddam posters in this village are camouflage, an attempt to protect the inhabitants from their Sunni neighbors, many of whom continue to support the ex-dictator. The Marsh Arabs are ecstatic that the Americans have come here, and they deluge Major Clark with requests for help: they have no money, no jobs, and they are surrounded by people who hate and despise them. Major Clark is taking notes as fast as he can, thinking up possible solutions on the fly and writing them down: "chicken farm and processing plant?" . . . "bus service into city" . . . "SCHOOL??" . . . These poor people and their problems are way beyond what CAT-A 13 can possibly handle, but at least Major Clark can pass them on to someone who can, and should (but probably won't, no matter how many times Major Clark chivies them). One good thing: just by visiting the Marsh Arabs the team has informed the neighboring villages that the U.S. knows of their existence, that they are on the Army's radar, and that will give them a measure of protection. "Can't go hassle those damned Swamp Shi'as now that the infidels talked to them."

All too soon it's time to leave; the team is already running late for the DAC. We race out to the highway and weave our way back to downtown al-Khadimiyah, Cruddas at the wheel of the lead Hummer driving like a demon, blissed out because for once he is free to use his L.A. road-racing skills. For all his efforts, we arrive at the DAC twenty minutes late; but then it turns out the meeting the Major was hurrying to make has been called off because none of the Iraqis showed up. So we drive back up to al-Shula and spend the rest of the day checking out the sewage disaster there: broken and blocked sewer lines have flooded streets and empty lots, turning them into stinking morasses.

Another day, a typical round of missions: checking on the restoration of the Baghdad Gate, visiting the District Advisory Council so Major Clark can pay contractors, and Grundman and Paul can attend the DAC Security Committee meeting (the committee members want weapons permits, so they can carry handguns to defend themselves) and then searching for soccer field sites all over the neighborhood. Someone in the Big Army has decided that what Iraqis need is more sports facilities and playgrounds: he's probably thinking of the after-school basketball programs in our own inner cities, which stop kids from getting in trouble by keeping them busy shooting hoops. A little different from the situation here, where teenagers are blowing up themselves, other teenagers and American soldiers in their spare time; but the CAT-A 13 members have discussed it and decided that it really can't hurt: in today's Iraq, anything good is worth doing.

The Major has directions to several prospective athletic fields, big empty lots that will be converted into soccer pitches by cleaning up the rocks and debris, laying out boundary lines and erecting goals and small, austere concrete bleachers for spectators. The second one we go looking for is evasive: we end up driving through narrower and narrower streets, where the bulky Humvees have to maneuver back and forth repeatedly to turn around. CAT-A 13 hasn't been in this area before, and it is clear that the people here don't get many American visitors: old men stop, do double-takes and stare; kids yell excitedly and chase the convoy; housewives peer from the doors of their compounds, laughing and whispering to each other.

Finally we find a neighborhood school; the prospective soccer field is right behind it, a hardscrabble expanse littered with broken glass and stones. Major Clark and Sergeant Paul go into the school to talk with the teachers and get their input on the project, while the rest of the team waits outside in the two Humvees.

Almost immediately a crowd of kids, mostly elementary school boys and girls, with a sprinkling of older youths, are all yelling, screaming, asking the soldiers' names, wanting their pictures taken, begging for *chocolata*. At first they are just enthusiastic, laughing, trying out their English, jostling to get in close. The two women on the team, Espi and Lynn, are the biggest attraction: every little girl wants to hug them, and little boys shout "I love you" and proposals of marriage. But as the crowd gets larger and larger, the kids become almost hysterical. Women at the edge hustle their sons and daughters away. A couple of teenaged boys shout at the others to calm down and back off, but no one listens.

Finally Fat Larry radios the Major and Sergeant Paul, who are still inside the school, and tells them it is time to go: we don't want the smaller kids to get trampled, or fighting to break out. The Major and Sergeant Paul appear a minute later, shake hands with the teachers they have been talking to, squeeze through the mob to the Humvees and get in. The drivers start their engines, and the team pulls out, circling back to exit across the empty field. There are deafening cheers, shrieks and shouts from the crowd, and then, as we reach the far end of the field, a volley of rocks comes flying. I am in back of the second vehicle with SAW-gunner Kramer, and I watch as a rock the size of a softball arcs toward us, getting bigger and bigger, till it whistles between our heads, missing us both by less than two feet. More rocks clang off the vehicle bodies, bounce and clatter around inside the open backs. We swerve around the corner of a building into the safety of an alleyway, and keep accelerating away.

By some absolute miracle no one has been hurt, though Grundman had a missile glance off his body armor. The larger rocks were big enough to kill someone if one struck them in the head.

We stop a mile or so farther on to regroup. Everyone is talking:

"I knew we stayed there too long," Grundman complains.

"It wasn't the little kids," Espi says. "It was some bigger boys, who snuck into the back of the crowd."

"I don't think they were mad or anything; they just got too excited," Fat Larry opines.

"Yeah?" says Cruddas. "Well, I'd hate to see the little bastards when they're mad."

"We'll chalk that one up to experience," Major Clark says. "It was my fault. Obviously I lost track of the time, and we stayed there way too long. If it starts to happen again, someone get on the radio right away and tell me to get out of there."

We drive on.

We have just found the next site, an empty area big enough for three or four soccer fields, when another convoy of eight or nine Humvees pulls up behind us at the curb. They are from a newly deployed unit of Combat Engineers; they are trying to find the airport, and they are completely lost, nowhere near it. Their onboard GPSes are down, and they don't know the geography of Baghdad at all. It is also getting late: if they don't find their way soon, they are going to end up driving around Baghdad at night, easy prey for the ambushers and bombers.

CAT-A 13 was supposed to go by the al-Khadimiyah maintenance yard, where they are paying a contractor to build new dorms for the guards, but the Major decides we can't leave the Engineers to find the airport on their own. He has them fall in behind us, and we drive across Baghdad till we reach the on-ramp for one of the freeways leading out to BIAP. He gives the convoy leader a final set of directions—keep going past al-Mansur, don't take the Abu Ghraib exit by mistake, till you see the signs for the airport—and we watch them till they are on the ramp entering the freeway. Then we hang a U-turn, jump the median and head back to Banzai.

The bottom line always remains that CA troops never really know what they are going to be doing or what is going to happen to them when they head out in the morning.

8

MEANWHILE THE WAR continues to heat up around us. Ever since my third day with the team, when we stumbled into the Mehdi Army over in east Baghdad, the violence all across Iraq has steadily increased. The 425th's presence in Baghdad has been ransacked to try and cope with the Mehdi Army uprising in the south. Half the battalion, including Doc Watters's Public Health Team, is yanked from its ongoing missions here and sent down to the Shi'a Triangle to revive Civil Affairs operations there as 1st Cav, 1st AD and Marine units try to restore order. From the reports we hear they are doing their usual good job, but this isn't really how Civil Affairs is supposed to work: CA is all about continuity, building up personal relationships and building long-lasting institutions that will survive far into the future, and you can't do that when you use CA teams as QRFs, Quick Reaction Forces, plugging them in wherever things get bad and then pulling them out and sending them somewhere else as the fortunes of war shift.

And now even al-Khadimiyah itself is threatened by large-scale fighting. One night Sadr Brigade fighters take over one of the local police stations in al-Mansur and surround one of our friendly sheikhs in his house. A 1/5 Cav force is sent to the rescue, only to be ambushed on its way there. We sit around the team house monitoring the radio, listening helplessly as our comrades in arms fight for survival and another armored column is rushed to save them; a one-act tragedy, broken up by volleys of static and the sound of gunfire.

"Knight Mike, this is Mike-6. We're taking RPGs and small arms fire from the north side of Sector 45, over."

"Mike 6, this is Knight Mike. The QRF reports it is now three hundred meters east of your current location, over."

"I have one Kilo India Alpha and two Whiskey India Alpha, and one Bradley down. Tell the QRF not, repeat not, to advance further till we suppress hostile fire, there are Bad Guys along their approach route, over."

"Understood. Do you require a 1-5-0 medevac for your Whiskey India Alphas? Over."

"That's a negative on the 1-5-0—WIA are still mission capable"—a muffled explosion—"Update as situation—"

"Roger that—ah—"

By dawn the police station is reoccupied and the sheikh rescued, but at least one U.S. soldier is dead and several more wounded. When the convoys return to Banzai, we see one Bradley fighting vehicle that has been literally torn asunder by RPG hits at the base of the turret, and another scorched, ripped, its treads knocked loose.

Over the next week things get worse and worse. The two interpreters, al-Janabi and Ajay, have disappeared, and Major Clark tells me privately that he thinks they are dead: Iraqis who work for the Americans are being hunted down and killed everywhere. When we drive to the Green Zone to try to hire someone to fill in for them, we find a long line of Iraqis at the Titan subcontracting office, which provides interpreters and translators for the Army and CPA. They are all desperate for work, in spite of the dangers—unemployment is so omnipresent and interpreters' salaries so high by postwar Iraqi standards that educated Iraqis compete fiercely for empty positions—but when Major Clark tells them they will be working in al-Khadimiyah they all bow out: evidently they know something we don't.

The war closes in around Banzai. One night we are in the team house monitoring the radios when we hear an explosion across the river; a few seconds later a voice on the radio reports, "We just had an RPG fired at a helicopter."

Over the next few hours Bad Guys overrun the main police station in Adhamiyah, the hard-core Sunni district to our south, on the east bank of the Tigris. The 1st Armored Battalion stationed there comes roaring out of their forward patrol base, Gunner Palace, and are immediately hit by daisy-chained IEDs and insurgents firing RPGs from rooftops and alleyways. The Tet Offensive must have been something like this.

The people of al-Khadimiyah are still friendly, but outsiders keep coming in to incite the dissatisfied minority. Gunmen attack Banzai every night, firing on the gate guards, and we get hit with mortar rounds as well. A group of Bad Guys attempts to infiltrate the post by sneaking along the unfenced riverbank; they are sighted by sentries with night vision scopes and driven off. Cav patrols and combat engineers pulling night sweeps along likely IED danger zones have to fight their way back to Banzai.

Blackhawks cruise the Tigris every night, as gunfire crackles around the perimeter of Banzai, and mortar rounds and rockets hit here and there. Two or three Cav troops are wounded when a mortar shell impacts on the basketball court beside the TOC; one officer has to be medevacked to Germany and on to the States. The hajji shops on the post close every few days because the employees are too frightened to come to work, and the Internet and outside phones shut down for twenty-four hours every time Cav troops are killed or wounded, so the word doesn't reach home before families are notified. We feel more and more isolated.

One day at the DAC, while Major Clark is inside attending a meeting, Sergeant Paul decides we should stroll down to one of the sidewalk cafes in the neighborhood and eat lunch. He goes in and bounces the idea off the Major, who considers for about half a second and then grins and says, "Sure."

We troop out the gate before the astonished Iraqi guards. "Where are you going?" the young guy we call Louie asks.

"Getting something to eat," Sergeant Paul says.

Louie stares, then laughs and gives us a thumbs-up.

Seven of us, toting our weapons casually, saunter across the street and head north along the riverfront highway. Traffic speeds by, vehicles swerving at the unimaginable sight of American soldiers strolling down a Baghdad sidewalk, talking and laughing among themselves, apparently oblivious to our surroundings (though we are watching for trouble out of the corners of our eyes, and my right hand is in my pocket, holding my trusty .38 revolver ready). A black-clad woman and a little boy approach. When they first see us, a look of horror crosses their faces—they obviously think they have stumbled into a combat patrol out on some antiterrorist sweep—but as we draw closer and they see our casual air and total lack of concern, the mother smiles and says something to her son, and we all say hello as we pass. A couple of kids hotrodding by on an Opel yell, and when we look over they are waving thumbs-up fists back at us.

Sergeant Paul begins to get into it, relishing the scene: the combat arms troops in lockdown or convoying at high speed with guns pointing everywhere, and here is this little CA team *walking to lunch.* When we reach the first cafe, he checks out the roasted chickens rotating on their spits, shakes his head and says, "Let's try the next one"; there's nothing really wrong here, but he's playing the gourmet, looking for the best possible dining experience, war or no war. What effing war? We check out two or three more—we're now four or five long blocks from the DAC, which is way out of sight around the curve behind us. Finally we settle on a cafe with a big shady outdoor dining area right on the road; the proprietor and his cohorts are all smiles as we seat ourselves at one of the long tables. Grundman radios back to the DAC, checking in: "Rogue 6, this is Grundman. We have found lunch, over."

The Major's voice, obviously amused, comes crackling back: "Roger that. Hey, be sure and bring some food back for the rest of the team."

"Rogue 6, that's an affirmative. Over."

"Should we eat here or get carryout?" someone asks Sergeant Paul.

Paul leans back in his chair expansively. "Let's eat here. I hate the fucking DAC."

We order everything the cafe has: roasted chickens, yogurt, salad, hummus, peppers and sheaves of that terrific Iraqi bread, so much that the proprietor has to send one of the waiters to the cafe next door to get more, with cans of soda to wash it down. While we gorge ourselves, more Iraqis show up to enjoy the sight of American soldiers enjoying themselves. A stout old matron driving a battered sedan pulls up to the curb and just sits there grinning at us, while to our amazement the three absolutely gorgeous young women she is chauffering whisper conspiratorially and then begin smiling at us and winking.

"Hey, that one's flirting with me," Cruddas says.

"She doesn't even notice you, Cruddas," Grundman scoffs. "Anyone can see she's flirting with *me*. She wants Grundman. The old lady's already picked you out for herself."

Cruddas turns to me. "Hey, Writer Rob, is she looking at me or Grundman?"

"Neither. They've all been looking right at me ever since they got here."

"I hate to tell you guys, but when a girl laughs at you she isn't flirting, she just thinks you look like an idiot," Sergeant Paul says.

Meanwhile more cars drive by honking their approval, and the restaurant owner keeps asking, "Everything is good? Everything is good?" When we assure him his food is delicious, he beams like a lighthouse, only to ask us again two minutes later, as if he can't hear it enough. It's lunchtime in Nirvana for one and all.

We finally head back to the DAC, lugging carryout food for the guys who stayed behind. "Rogue 6, this is Rogue 5 1/2, returning to the DAC, mission accomplished. Over."

"Affirmative. What happened to Rogue 5, 5 1/2?"

"Rogue 5 ate so much he added half a number, Rogue 6. Over and out."

Word must have spread about the Ameriki soldiers dining
out in al-Khadimiyah: traffic has doubled or tripled since we arrived at the cafe, with every kind of vehicle imaginable driving
by in both directions, horns honking, people yelling, waving,
cheering. Kids on bicycles, a whole covey of them, cruise past,
voices chirruping, *"Mistah good! Mistah good! Mistah good!"*
The soldiers beam and wave at their admirers like the honorary
Kings of al-Khadimiyah as they saunter back to the DAC.

The team's insouciance is more than just styling: an important though unwritten part of their mission is to help establish a
feeling of normalcy in the AO.

One afternoon Major Clark returns from a meeting at the
Cav TOC and reports that Banzai is going into 100 percent lock-
down; Colonel Miyamasu is expecting a mass assault on the
FOB tonight.

The CAT-A 13 compound is about twenty yards from Banzai's vulnerable northeastern corner. Across the perimeter road a
lone guard tower looks out over the barbed wire–topped concrete wall into a tract of palm-tree plantation; in the past gunmen
have approached through the palm trees under cover of night to
fire into the post. There is a gap of about thirty feet where the
wall meets the Tigris; the Cav usually stations a group of sentries
there after dark, but just to be sure Major Clark, Grundman,
Cruddas and I drag a coil of razor wire over there and stake it out
across the hole. That doesn't cover the whole east side of Banzai
bordered by the river, where there are no walls or wire at all, but
the Cav has that protected with night vision gear, Bradleys and
heavy machine guns. A good thing, because the Tigris is so low

insurgents could probably wade across it from the hostile neighborhoods on the opposite shore.

The team also has to prepare for the possibility that enemy forces will break through and they will end up defending the CAT-A compound itself.

Everyone has to hurry, as it is getting late; the sun is already setting. We climb onto the roof, up the shaky iron ladder on the side of the house. Someone, probably one of the Iraqi Army officers who once lived here, has left a dozen or so sandbags and some bricks lying around up there, and we throw together a couple of knee-high firing positions. Kramer is put in charge of the rooftop, and he hauls a SAW-gun up there and places it so it covers the front of the compound. Fat Larry, Goff and I will cover the rest of the 360 degrees.

"What if we have to haul ass out of here?" Fat Larry asks.

Kramer looks over the front of the building; just below is the corrugated sheet metal roof over the front door, with the Humvees parked in the driveway just beyond. "We jump down onto the tin roof, slide down into the Humvee, and we're outta here." Kramer grins; I think he actually relishes the thought. We climb down into the yard and reassemble, and Major Clark points out firing positions for Espi and Cruddas at the front corners of the house. Back in the office, Sergeant Paul gets out the night vision gear and Grundman does a commo check, making sure the radios are working. People check their M-16 and 9mm handgun clips. Major Clark walks out, closes the front gates to the compound and latches them. "Now don't go and fire up the first person who comes to the gate," he says when he returns. "It'll probably be someone from the Cav, checking on us. We don't want any friendly fire incidents."

"Yeah, *Cruddas*," Fat Larry says, elbowing him.

"Yeah, *Fat Larry*," Cruddas says, elbowing him back.

Sergeant Paul looks at them both and shakes his head. "Now I really feel safe," he says sarcastically.

"You should," Cruddas says. "Hey, I'll pile the bodies up so high Kramer'll be able to walk down off the roof on 'em."

A few minutes later he and Espi go out to check the dead ground on the far side of the old air raid shelter, where attackers could take cover. On the way back he boasts to Espi about his skill in hand-to-hand combat; she replies by laughing and flipping him to the ground. He pulls her on top of him, and they grapple together ferociously. Cruddas and Espi are like rowdy siblings: there's no sexuality to any of this, just a couple of kids who like joking around and giving each other a hard time. The impromptu match ends when Espi gets Cruddas in a submission hold she learned in Airborne training, twisting his wrist behind his back till he begs for mercy.

Sergeant Paul watches it all with a bemused expression.

"What was it the British general said when someone asked him about his soldiers, if he thought they frightened the enemy? 'I don't know about the enemy, but they sure scare the hell out of me.' "

After a while, the night quiets down; we wait in an eerie silence, broken only by the occasional barking and howling of the wild dogs out in the palm plantation.

By midnight the CAT-A 13 soldiers have gotten tired of waiting for the apocalypse and are keeping themselves occupied with various arcane pursuits.

Fat Larry has noticed a section of the tile floor in the office that looks vaguely like a trapdoor: the cracks between the tiles

form a rough square around two feet on a side. He decides for
some reason that there is a secret chamber beneath the building
that contains either a fortune in gold (the movie *Three Kings* is a
favorite among CA troops) or a subterranean torture chamber;
he enlists Kramer, and soon the two of them are chiseling away
at the tiles, trying to uncover the hidden door. Major Clark has
gone over to the TOC to check on the security situation, and
when the cat's away the mice will play. Sergeant Paul encourages
them to keep going. His motives are purely mischievous: he
takes me aside and tells me quietly he is sure there is nothing
down there under the tiles, but he wants to see the Major's face
when he returns and finds his office floor torn up. The sarge
loves a good joke, especially if it is inflicted on Fat Larry.

Meanwhile Grundman is holed up on his bunk, painstakingly answering letters from schoolkids back home; dozens of
them have written him, and instead of writing one letter back to
the whole class he is writing each of them individually. "They
deserve it," he tells me. "They're all great kids." After he finishes
with that, he is going to write the weekly column that he does,
free of charge, for his hometown paper.

To everyone's relief, Ajay and al-Janabi show up again. They
survived the last two weeks by lying low. Al-Janabi is an important figure in the al-Janabi tribe, and he lives in a neighborhood
where almost all his neighbors are fellow tribesmen: he smiles as
he tells us, "Anyone who comes to my street looking for me had
better be a friend." Ajay is less forthcoming about where he hid
out, but I imagine a room full of carryout pizza boxes, beer cans
and overflowing ashtrays, a large-screen television playing *Victo-*

ria's Secret TV specials, and a whole platoon of Ajay clones playing liar's dice, seven-card stud and South Texas fetch and phoning up friends and acquaintances at three A.M.: "Is Mullah Nasruddin there?" (Mullah Nasruddin being the mythical archetypal Sufi joker.)

The traffic circle parks are going in under Espi's supervision; Sergeant Paul's big project to restore the ornamental tiles and brickwork on the monumental Ottoman-era Baghdad Gate, and put in gardens and a playground: it is looking beautiful. The Taji sanitary landfill, which will help clean up the whole northwestern quadrant of Baghdad, is up and running, complete with recycling zones for different kinds of material, high earthen berms surrounding it, and even a little strip of lawn out front with saplings and a sprinkler rotating away, keeping it green. The best of the Iraqi contractors the team hires take real pride in their work and don't cut corners; they seem to view themselves as more than profit-taking businessmen, as an important part of the rebirth of their nation. They often bring their children with them to their job sites, to show them a piece of the Iraq they will inherit.

On the negative side, the residents of al-Shula are still complaining about their sewage problem, blaming it on us, even though the pipes were laid during the Saddam era and they broke because the contractor cheated and used an inferior product. Not only that, the clogged lines are backed up because thieves stole the manhole covers and other Iraqis came along and used the holes as handy trash receptacles, stuffing garbage, brush, even pieces of broken furniture down them.

The new manhole covers the team ordered have arrived, but they are currently sitting in a municipal compound in central al-Khadimiyah because the people there don't like their brethren in al-Shula and can't be bothered to deliver the covers to them. Meanwhile the al-Shula people keep trying to blow up the big sewage processing plant that is located in their neighborhood, which makes no sense because it would drastically exacerbate the very problems they ceaselessly complain about. If they ever do succeed, they won't have to worry about missing manhole covers anymore; they'll have to hire the Marsh Arabs to carve them up a fleet of *taradas* (native Iraqi swamp boats) so they can float around their neighborhood on a sea of seething excrement.

The last time the team went to al-Shula, it was to look at ways of improving the neighborhood's ramshackle bazaar: Major Clark has a vision, of a clean, neat marketplace, moved back from the busy highway with plenty of room to park. "If the bazaar were fixed up, people from outside the neighborhood might stop by and shop. Al-Shula could use the added income." Perhaps, but it seems like a lot of folks in al-Shula are more interested in killing Kafirs than in civic improvements. Major Clark, three other team members and I had just finished walking the length of the bazaar, interviewing merchants and shoppers, and were mired in a crowd of grinning youths who just wouldn't move. One of the rotund old black-clad Shi'a grandmothers who patrol the bazaar had just come along and driven the mob away with a volley of earsplitting oaths, when Sergeant Paul got an emergency message from the two SAW-gunners back on the Humvees. Something had struck them as not right: the looks on the faces of passersby, the way traffic sped up as it passed, some nameless vibe—simultaneously they trained their SAW-guns on the roofline of the nearest building, just in time to see two men with AK-47s appear at the edge of the roof, obviously hoping for a free shot at the team. When they saw the two SAWs pointed right up at them, with the glaring eyes of Kramer and Grundman behind, they vanished like smoke, but the gunners want to get out of here, and fast. We double-time back to the Humvees and leave.

It is obvious what was going on in the marketplace: the crowd that suddenly materialized around us was supposed to delay us while the gunmen on the rooftop took out the troops on the Humvees; then they would either swarm over us with knives, or toss a grenade in our midst. If it wasn't for the good-hearted old Shi'a lady and two very alert SAW-gunners, we wouldn't be alive. Things like that are always happening in al-Shula, but it still gives you a sick, dizzy feeling in the pit of your stomach. How many of the smiling faces that plead for sewer repairs or a new pedestrian walkover for schoolchildren are secretly dreaming of a bomb beneath the Humvee, a sniper team on the rooftop, a crowd with butcher knives and rebar killing clubs hidden beneath their shirts?

But to Major Clark, there's no friend like an enemy in need, as someone on the team recently put it. When he hears there are five brand-new hydraulic sewer cleaning trucks stashed at the al-Shula wastewater plant, he is overjoyed: here is the perfect answer to al-Shula's problems. Everybody drops what they are doing, and the team heads back up to al-Shula at high speed. There is a side road off the main highway just before the bazaar; it leads through a dusty field, past the twisted and shattered hulks of Iraqi howitzers and triple-A guns left over from the battle for Baghdad. The plant is surrounded by earthen berms and barbed wire fences, and a half dozen Iraqi rent-a-guards with AKs man the gate. They aren't an impressive lot: we honk and shout repeatedly before they tumble out of the sentry shack, and one drops his weapon on his foot to the amusement of his buddies as another shammer with a great effort drags the gate open.

And there the trucks are, parked in a neat row beside the main building: five expensive, shiny red made-in-Italy trucks, built to unclog the most stubborn sewer pipeline with ease. The customs receipts are still taped to the windows. Kramer, the team's resident mechanic, gets in the nearest one and checks it out: the key is in the ignition, and it fires right up.

It looks like the people of al-Shula are in business, if Major Clark and his soldiers survive long enough to put the trucks to work.

9

CAT-A 13 HAS definitely been pushing it, ever since the traffic circle encounter with the Mehdi Army. A lot of units pulled back during the worst of the fighting, postponing long trips outside the wire and canceling all but the most important missions. Major Clark and company just kept going and, as in the case of the Marsh Arab village, even went way beyond their official mission list. Major Clark and Sergeant Paul in particular would much rather be rolling, Condition Red or not, than be hanging around Banzai, the Green Zone or BIAP/Victory.

"I didn't come over here to waste a year of my life filling out paperwork," Sergeant Paul has told me. And Major Clark sometimes comes out with half-joking lines like "Let's go up to Sobiabor and see if we can get anyone to shoot at us."

Civil Affairs teams often end up spending more time out in the field than other kinds of troops, because that is where their work is, and CAT-A 13 definitely is way, way above average in hours spent in the field. On the positive side, they seem to be the best CA team in the 425th as far as combat skills are concerned. Clark and Kramer are as good as it gets, and you can tell both Sergeant Paul and Grundman would come through with flying colors in an ambush or firefight situation. When the whole team took the combat shooting skills test at a firing range outside Baghdad, which involved shooting at targets while driving at high speeds and carrying out a mock first aid and medevac drill, they scored higher than almost any other unit in the Baghdad area, including the hard-core combat arms guys.

The thing about Iraq is, survival here isn't always a matter of skill; luck plays a huge role, because of the nature of the conflict. If your Humvee drives past an IED or runs into a suicide car bomber you'll be burned toast. And the more hours and miles you put in out beyond the wire, the more the odds are against you. I think about it a lot.

And what I have feared finally happens.

I have returned to BIAP for a couple of days, to visit with Colonel Kelly and pick up some gear I left at my friend Major Pilot's hooch.

From the vantage point of Banzai, BIAP and Victory seem like REMF territory, home to desk jockeys and pencil-pushing geeks, but now that I'm back here I realize the new war is hitting here too, hitting hard. The first day I'm back, rockets start falling on the airfield in broad daylight, and they just keep coming. As Major Pilot and I are driving through the east side of BIAP, another one nearly nails the big fuel dump there; the Filipino contract employees who work there scatter in all directions. If a missile hit those tanks and sprawling swimming pool–sized fuel bladders, the whole area would go up in a mammoth fireball.

This evening all of BIAP goes on Red Alert: shades of Banzai three nights ago. An intel report has come in stating that the insurgents are planning a mass assault on BIAP, and the 425th troops still based at the airport go into circle-the-wagons mode. Pilot, his roommate Colonel Lattamore and I set up a schedule of rotating watches on the roof, armed with M-16s and handguns; if the Bad Guys make it over the outer wall, which is just across the road, whoever is awake is supposed to yell an alert and start shooting. Far from being nervous, Pilot and Lattamore act like the whole thing is a lark. "It was getting boring around here anyway," Pilot says. "And I wouldn't mind shooting a couple of these terrorist types. I'd be doing the Iraqi people a favor." I end up sleeping through the night: Lattamore and Pilot are having so much fun on guard duty they don't wake me up for my watches.

Not all of the 425th's headquarters types are as coolheaded as my two friends. Frank O'Doule (not his real name), finicky, neurotic officer from the TOC, recruits one of the 425th's female officers, Mary Anne Musswell (also a pseudonym) and the two set out on a foot patrol at dawn. It's a sure prescription for disaster: the other day O'Doule mistook a backfire for a gunshot, and told everyone al-Qaeda had infiltrated BIAP, while Musswell is so nervous she's been sleeping in her shower enclosure in underwear, body armor, helmet and boots, her M-16 in her lap. During their dawn patrol the squirrely pair see a young man jogging in a gray Army T-shirt and shorts. This is prescribed PT garb, but for some reason they decide the jogger looks suspicious, and they challenge him, asking him for the day's password. As Pilot says later, not only didn't he know the daily password, he wasn't even aware there *was* one. When the poor guy says he doesn't know, O'Doule and Musswell point their weapons at him; according to eyewitnesses, Musswell is screaming hysterically, threatening to open fire, and O'Doule is shaking so hard he nearly drops his 9mm. The jogger is so terrified he defecates in his shorts. An officer in a Humvee shows up just in time and takes charge; while he rails at the two heroes, the jogger excuses himself and runs for the nearest outhouse.

Nothing happened at BIAP that night, but the war is definitely still going on everywhere else. That morning Pilot, Lattamore and I drive over to the 82nd Airborne chow hall for breakfast and park next to a row of trucks that has just arrived on a supply run from Kuwait. They have clearly had a tough trip: several of the trucks have shattered windshields, and there are bullet holes in some of the trailers. A tall jet-black woman with high cheekbones and fine-chiseled Hamitic features climbs down from the cab of the nearest rig; the seat behind her is sticky with blood and littered with shards of glass.

"Bad trip, huh?" Colonel Lattamore asks her.

"Yes, sir," she says. "It always is."

"Anyone badly hurt?" Major Pilot is staring at the broken glass and blood.

"No, not bad. I was driving when the windshield got busted, and the glass missed me and hit my buddy. He just got cut up, is all." She points with a slight movement of her head, indicating a freckled kid with strawberry-red hair sitting on an ammo can in the dust, one side of his face swathed in dirty bandages. He looks up at us: "You get cut in the face, it bleeds like a motherfucker, sir," he says. "Ain't nothin'."

The truck crews have painted insults and charms in white paint on their dingy brown vehicles: a cartoon pig in a turban, over the words "EAT MORE PORK," a grinning Satan with a pitchfork, "Fuck Iraq," "Don't Shoot, You're Momma's In Here," "Bewear Road Warriors Rule," "WHOS YOUR BAGH-DADDY NOW?" Normally the MPs who guard the gates at BIAP, Victory and the Green Zone bust military vehicles with unauthorized graffiti, but these words and images look old, like they've survived many months, many miles. Lattamore, Pilot and I talk about it, and we agree that only the most chickenshit MP would screw with the truckers who do the Kuwait-to-Baghdad supply run. If these defiant voodoo scrawls somehow give them an edge, ward off evil, then leave them alone, let them be.

On my second night at BIAP Major Clark calls: the team is driving over first thing in the morning on a mail and supply run to the A-LOC, and they'll pick me up. I tell him I'm more than ready to go; I can't wait to get back to Banzai, the team house and al-Khadimiyah.

At eight the next morning the CAT-A 13 convoy heads over from Banzai: three Humvees, six of the CAT-A 13 regulars and three or four headquarters troops who have just finished a week-long deployment with the team. Major Clark has stayed behind at Banzai to take care of some paperwork.

Just after nine I check my watch and see that the team is over-due. I walk over from Pilot's hooch to the A-LOC carrying my baggage with me. I figure they'll be in a hurry to get back to Banzai, and I'll save them a few minutes by meeting them there. As I walk in the door, a message is coming in over the radio: a convoy en route to BIAP on Route Irish has just been hit with an IED. "Shit, somebody got it," I exclaim, to nobody in particular. Sergeant Venters shakes his head grimly: "Route Irish again."

A second later Major Pilot bursts in, his cell phone to his ear. "That convoy that hit the IED—it's our guys. Major Clark's team."

"What?" At times like this your mind goes blank momentarily before it coughs up the answer it already knows; a last brief interval of grace before you have to deal with what you don't want to.

Major Pilot is still listening to someone on the phone; he switches it off and says, "They've taken them to the med center at Victory."

Pilot has one of 425th HQ's old SUVs today, and he and I pile in. We head over to Victory as fast as traffic and the MPs will allow. The whole way Pilot stays on the phone, trying to find out exactly what happened. It sounds like no one is dead, but at least one soldier is wounded, maybe more. A wave of irrational guilt sweeps over me: why wasn't I there? I feel like I have betrayed them somehow. The one time they are attacked I wasn't there. I don't know what you can do about an IED, but maybe I would have seen something, spotted the IED before it went off, *something*. All the way over to Victory—and the trip seems to take forever—I rip myself up and down and inside out: my friends got hit, and I was somewhere else.

We finally pull into the parking lot at the med shed, and there they are. Espi is hunched on the curb, head in her hands; Cruddas is sitting at the wheel of one of the Humvees, staring straight ahead, lifeless as a crash dummy. Sergeant Paul is on the radio. Fat Larry is handing a soda to Grundman. As Major Pilot and I get out and walk over to them, they look at us like we are men from Mars.

Inside, Goff is sitting in a chair, tears running down her face, while a nurse talks to her. She was driving the number two Humvee, the one that was hit, and she is complaining that her elbow hurts. But Kramer is the one who really got it. They have him lying on a cot, an IV in his arm. One knee is swollen up big as a softball, and the front of his thigh is opened up as if someone took an axe to it. His thumb is bandaged and splinted, and he holds it at an odd angle, as if he is afraid it's going to come off. He gives us one of his classic ferocious Kramer smiles, but when I look into his eyes I see a little kid, hurt, helpless and confused.

Later I talk to Sergeant Paul and reconstruct what happened. The three Humvees were approaching the Victory turnoff just before BIAP; Cruddas was driving the lead vehicle, with Paul as convoy commander next to him and Grundman up top on the SAW. One of the troops on temporary loan to us, the Russian-American kid we call KGB, was driving the number two, with Lieutenant Buenteo, another loaner, riding shotgun, and Espi on the SAW; Goff was driving the trail Humvee with Fat Larry next to her, and Kramer was manning the SAW, accompanied by Wheeler, another temporary team member.

The front of the convoy had just emerged from an underpass when there was a huge explosion. Sergeant Paul looked back, and past the second Humvee there was nothing, just an enormous bloom of dense black smoke. "I thought the third Humvee was gone, vaporized," Paul recollects. "We stopped, and I just kept looking back, and there was nothing. Meanwhile I was on the radio, calling in a situation report. Finally—it took over a minute and it felt like an eternity—the smoke cleared and I saw the third Humvee back there, crashed into the median barrier, the engine still running."

Sergeant Paul had Cruddas pull up another hundred meters in case another IED went off, and ran back to the rear of the convoy. "I was really proud of our guys," he tells me. "And Wheeler was great, too." (Wheeler is a commo expert and veteran of high-risk Special Ops missions in the Balkans and other war zones.) "Espi and someone else had checked Kramer's wounds and were loading him in the back of the second Humvee. Fat Larry had the rest of them spread in a three-hundred-and-sixty-degree defensive perimeter, just like they teach you in training, kneeling with their M-16s ready, and at the same time he was on one of the handhelds calling for backup."

It turns out Kramer had been hit by a piece of bomb shrapnel that went through the back of his helmet and sliced a shallow wound in his scalp; one more inch and he would have been killed. The shrap knocked him cold, just as the force of the blast blew him under the Humvee's tailgate, squeezing him through like toothpaste out of a tube. His unconscious body hit the tarmac at fifty-five miles an hour, and he bounced a hundred feet or so and came to rest in the middle of the road. The explosion also flung Goff out of the driver's seat—she wasn't wearing her seat belt—but she lucked out with just a banged-up elbow. The driverless vehicle swerved into the guardrail and stopped; it was scarred by shrapnel, battered and bent, but for all intents and purposes it made it through intact, a tribute to engineering and quality control.

Three days later Kramer is well enough to travel, and Major Clark leads his banged-up team back toward Banzai. We haven't gone a mile before three MP Humvees who happen to be ahead of us suddenly jam on their brakes just short of an overpass and peel off into a cloverleaf formation, blocking the road. A few seconds later more vehicles arrive on the scene, Humvees and Bradleys. Major Clark walks over and talks to the MP sergeant in charge, who points up to the roof of the overpass. The Major nods, and returns to the convoy. "There's four 155 rockets wired up under the overpass. They're set to explode down on whoever's driving through. The Engineers are on their way to defuse them."

I look around, at the houses shimmering in the sun, the palm trees, a couple of abandoned concrete huts in the highway median. I don't see a soul, but somewhere someone is watching us, a cell phone in his hand, ready to punch the button and set off the explosives. When a minute or two goes by and nothing happens, I take a deep breath and relax. The bomber must have spooked when he saw his bomb was discovered, and fled the scene . . . or else he is waiting to try to blow up the Engineers when they arrive; there's always that chance.

If we had been five or ten seconds earlier, we would be dead; our open-backed, unarmored Humvees would have made a perfect target. Especially with four 155s, crammed up where the wall and ceiling of the concrete overpass meet so the full force of the blast hits whoever is below.

Poor Kramer: he's just out of the hospital, and they're already trying to kill him again.

The MPs reroute traffic around the overpass, and we continue on our way home to Banzai.

As we roll down Irish, I realize suddenly how much I care about these people, Major Clark and his team. The IED was a revelation. Like Sergeant Paul, I really don't want to go home unless they—we—all do. Every day, 24/7, they've been looking out for me in a thousand ways I haven't noticed and they haven't given a second thought to it, and as long as I'm here I'm going to redouble my efforts to try and do the same for them. It's the least I can do.

*   *   *

The aftermath of the IED incident temporarily drives a wedge between CAT-A 13 and the 425. There's no malice or ill will involved, just misunderstanding and powerful emotions mishandled.

It seems that Kramer's M-16 disappeared when he was thrown out of the speeding Humvee. No doubt it was torn off its sling and battered into junk on the pavement, but someone at the TOC becomes obsessed with the idea it fell into the hands of the Bad Guys. They repeatedly question Sergeant Paul, the convoy commander, about why the weapon wasn't recovered.

The Rules of Engagement say that soldiers should exit the area as soon as possible after an IED explosion, in case there are more IEDs or the Bad Guys follow up the blast with AK-47s, RPGs and mortar fire; in point of fact this frequently happens, and we later learn that a Bradley sent to the scene after the CAT-A 13 vehicles left was hit by small-arms fire. But the TOC guys continue to harass Sergeant Paul with questions: "Did anyone see the M-16 after the IED went off?" "Did anyone go look for it?" "How hard did they look?"

It is sheer craziness. You would think they would put Sergeant Paul and the team in for a "mentioned in dispatches" commendation of some kind for their superb performance, but the battalion's only official response to the incident is to censure poor hapless Goff for not having her seat belt fastened. Then, to make things worse, Major Clark recommends that Kramer's deployment be terminated and he be sent home to fully recover. When that somehow doesn't happen, everyone on CAT-A 13 is furious. Here's Kramer, close to fifty years old, with a broken thumb, a concussion, an open flesh wound the length of his thigh, a wrenched back and a knee injury he may never recover from, ordered to return to active duty in the field. He can barely walk, even with the help of a cane, and there's no way he can climb up into a Humvee and man a SAW-gun, so for the next three weeks or so he busies himself rewiring the kitchen, tinkering with the faulty plumbing, doing carpentry repairs around the team house and cooking elaborate breakfasts and dinners for the team. He is in so much pain he can't lie down in bed; he spends nights curled up on the couch in the TV room, passing out for an hour or two at a time from sheer exhaustion. As he eloquently puts it, "I got fucked, and I didn't even get a kiss out of it."

Major Clark calls a team meeting in the TV room. He tells everyone that someone at the 425th TOC has come down on CAT-A 13 for "not acting like they're part of the battalion." The unnamed officer supposedly added, "Maybe we should just stop supplying them and they can be on their own from now on."

At that, everyone goes off. "Fuck them," Grundman says. "Who needs them, anyway?"

Cruddas grins. "Hey. If they don't want me anymore, that's fine, they can just send me home. I don't want to be here anyway."

"They were supporting us?" Fat Larry says. "Funny, I never noticed."

"I don't trust the Iraqi soldiers or the police," Sergeant Paul says. "I don't trust the DAC guards, and I definitely don't trust the Army. Now I don't trust anyone in the 425th either. As far as I'm concerned, the only people I'm gonna count on from now on is you guys."

"I guess we're outlaws now." Fat Larry laughs.

Afterward, Sergeant Paul, Grundman and I go outside to take in the nightly festival of explosions and gunfire across the river. "I came here thinking I was going to save Iraq," Sergeant Paul says quietly. "Now it's like I'm just putting in time till I go home, hoping nobody gets killed."

"Listen, for what it's worth I think you guys are doing a great job," I tell him.

"Thanks, Writer Rob. Be sure you spell my name right in the book."

Far away, over by Sadr City, the mosquito-like drone of a chopper is answered by the crackling sound of a heavy machine gun. Closer in, near the east bank of the Tigris, a loudspeaker rants and raves, exhorting the faithful to drive out the hated infidels. There is even something happening in the usually peaceful area to our southwest, around Hurriyah: a series of muffled explosions, probably a string of daisy-chained IEDs.

"So tell me again why we invaded Iraq," Grundman says.

The truth of the matter is, the IED incident has frightened everyone in the battalion. Kramer is one of the Old Reliables, and the fact that he is lucky to be alive now has freaked them out. So they've reacted irrationally, the way anyone would in a crazy place like Iraq, where even at BIAP the rockets and shells never stop falling and if you step outside the gate alone without a weapon you will be dead in an hour. Getting mad, focusing on nonsense like the missing M-16, these are ways of shutting out the fear, forgetting how close the battalion came to losing the beloved Kramer . . . and just how thin and fickle a thread life hangs from here.

No one who isn't here could imagine the stress these soldiers are under. There are dozens of bankruptcies, marriages folding and broken homes among the families of the fewer than two hundred members of the 425th. The first week I was in Baghdad, a young Asian-American soldier from the battalion was put on suicide watch and had his weapon taken away from him after his wife e-mailed and told him to forget about ever seeing her again. He was in Alpha Company's Internet room every night, either crying as he typed home or lying passed out from utter exhaustion, his head on the keyboard.

It doesn't help that back home the war is barely on the news, like Americans want to pretend it isn't happening; so they can go on with their lives undisturbed, watching *American Idol* and NASCAR. It is particularly hard to risk your life when you are nineteen or twenty years old and you aren't even a hero in the eyes of your nation. No wonder people here sometimes act crazy; actually, it's amazing how often they don't.

Major Clark has another one of his brainstorms. No one really has any idea if any of our CA programs or other attempts to help the Iraqis are paying off or not, so he writes up a questionnaire, to gauge Iraqi public opinion. Ajay and al-Janabi translate it into Arabic, four hundred copies are printed up, and the team distributes them around al-Khadimiyah.

The questionnaire is simple but incisive:

> WHAT NEIGHBORHOOD DO YOU LIVE IN?
> HOW OFTEN DOES YOUR NEIGHBORHOOD ADVISORY COUNCIL MEET?
> DOES THE KHADAMIYAH DG [DISTRICT GOVERNOR] DO A GOOD JOB MAINTAINING YOUR NEIGHBORHOOD?

*HAS THE CPA PREPARED IRAQIS TO PEACEFULLY GOV-
ERN THEIR COUNTRY?*

*WOULD YOU CONSIDER BECOMING A NAC [NEIGHBOR-
HOOD ADVISORY COUNCIL] OR DAC [DISTRICT ADVI-
SORY COUNCIL] MEMBER?*

[When we go over the questionnaire before distributing it, Sergeant Paul starts answering the questions aloud: "Yes. I could also take poison, or tie a four-hundred-kilo weight to my neck and jump headfirst into the Tigris."]

IS YOUR NEIGHBORHOOD SAFE FROM CRIME?

["Hey, someone stole my pencil!" Sergeant Paul jokes.]

*DO COALITION SOLDIERS WORK TO PROTECT YOUR FAM-
ILY?*

["They did, until we killed them all," Sergeant Paul says.]

ARE YOUR CHILDREN RECEIVING A GOOD EDUCATION?

IS YOUR FAMILY HEALTHY?

ARE YOU FREE TO TRAVEL ANYWHERE YOU WISH IN IRAQ?

[Sergeant Paul: "Yeah, I can't decide whether to spend my next holiday in Fallujah or Ramadi."]

*WHEN IRAQIS GOVERN IRAQ, WOULD YOU WELCOME VIS-
ITORS FROM OTHER COUNTRIES AND BE ABLE TO VISIT
FOREIGN COUNTRIES?*

ARE YOU ARE PROUD TO BE AN IRAQI?

Iraqis can choose from a range of five answers, from Very Positive to Very Negative. When the questionnaires come back, the results are pretty grim. Several Iraqis respond to the last question with the most negative Negative possible, and hardly anyone has a good thing to say about the NAC, DAC, CPA and DG. Clearly the team has a lot of work to do.

*   *   *

At the same time, it is clear that good things are happening, and the much-scorned fledgling civil government is a large contributing factor.

Government in Baghdad is a puzzle palace, a crossbred bastard stepchild sired by the CPA upon the old prewar Iraqi bureaucracy. There are small-scale advisory councils representing multi-block areas, NACs on top of that, and DACs whose representatives sit on the big all-Baghdad city council that meets periodically in the Green Zone and consults face to face with the CPA. Paralleling the advisory councils are various levels of professional administrators; Ibrahim Hamsa, the DG (Director General) of al-Khadimiyah, is a particularly bad example of this group. Think of it as the Iraqi equivalent of the mayor–city manager dichotomy in America.

The team spends a lot of time at the al-Khadimyah DAC, a heavily guarded compound half a mile upriver from Banzai on the main road to al-Shula, Taji and the Baghdad Gate. The DAC is set back from the road, surrounded by palm plantations; past the guardhouse a paved driveway leads back to a parking lot boxed in by two single-story office buildings. There is always something going on: security committee and women's meetings, public works contracts being signed, neighborhood politicos hobnobbing and plotting. Members of CAT-A 13 are the most frequent U.S. military visitors, spending time there almost every day, but Cav officers from Banzai and Camp Victory also show up regularly. When things are busy, the parking lot is jammed with Humvees: Colonel Formica never makes the trip from Victory with fewer than four or five Humvees for security, sometimes as many as seven. He, Major Clark, Colonel Miyamasu and company hole up for hours inside the main meeting room while scores of soldiers cook outside in the sun, the SAW-gunners lolling behind their weapons, troops strolling the fence lines with M-16s, and others on the rooftops keeping an eye on the main road. Cav and CA soldiers renew old acquaintances, joke around with the Iraqi guards or heat up MREs. Whoever said that war was 99 percent excruciating boredom and discomfort and 1 percent unbearable terror had it about right. Some days seem to go on forever and ever.

The Iraqis who come to the DAC are an endlessly varied bunch. The regulars, the businessmen and politicians drawn irresistibly to this nexus of money, power and influence, range from sophisticated young wheeler-dealers in suits and ties to bearded tribal sheikhs in white robes and Shi'a clerics in black.

The CAT-A 13 troops have gotten to know many of them. Sheikh Mektub, for instance, a distinguished-looking graybeard who is always immaculately clad and inevitably shows up with a retinue of cronies and hangers-on. He seems like the essence of the dignified Arab desert chief, but like all too many Iraqis in official positions, he is widely suspected of graft and influence peddling by his fellow countrymen. And then comes the day he shows up rubbing his rear end and complaining loudly to the other Iraqis that his boyfriend was too enthusiastic in bed the night before and that he isn't sure he will be able to sit down in the upcoming meeting. When some of the DAC guards translate the drift of Mektub's patter, Sergeant Paul grimaces, Grundman nearly chokes on his Skoal, and Cruddas gives a howl of outrage—"No, no, I don't want to know!"—putting his hands over his ears. From that day on it is difficult to look the sheikh in the eye, and Cruddas makes a dramatic show of backing up against the wall protectively whenever he walks by.

To be fair, the sheikh isn't typical of the Iraqis who serve on the DAC committees and make neighborhood policy. Habib, a young Shi'a auto mechanic who serves on the security committee along with Grundman, is painfully honest and very, very sharp. And then there is Hussein, the roly-poly Shi'ite mullah who also sits on the security board: I find myself wishing all those pundits back home who go on endlessly about "fanatical" Moslems who are genetically programmed for hatred and homicidal violence could meet this jolly little man who greets every American he sees with a huge smile and a loud greeting. It isn't safe to be overfriendly to the infidel invaders here in Iraq; it can get you killed—more than one DAC member has been murdered since CAT-A 13 arrived on the scene—but the mullah doesn't seem to care at all. These Iraqi Shi'ites, at least those I've met, are the real deal, old school Moslems who still follow the traditions of hospitality, tolerance and kindness to strangers.

The everyday citizens, who come here seeking jobs, lobbying for neighborhood improvements or lodging complaints, represent every level of Iraqi society. Here is a rotund old matron swathed in black, like a human bowling ball, chaperoning her willowy daughter or granddaughter who is looking for a secretarial job; the younger woman giving a sly sidelong smile as they go out the gate, earning an admonitory punch in the shoulder from Grandma, who undoes her dragon act a moment later as she too looks back and gives us a mischievous grin. Here comes a group of five young men, wise guys in flashy polyester shirts (one wears a Manchester United long-sleeved tee), joking and jiving as they walk by. They are here to visit an older brother who works at the DAC, but you can tell they really just want to check out the scene, sneaking glances at us and trading whispers. Cruddas, always genuinely friendly, waves to them and calls, "Hey, motherfucker, whuzzappening?" They hesitate and then come over, and soon Cruddas is teaching them gang handshakes and daps; the teenagers are nearly writhing in ecstasy, transfused with actual American Hipness. An ancient sheikh from the sticks stops to bum a cigarette from Cruddas and a hit of Skoal from me; when I offer him the open tin, he takes a pinch, then replaces the lid, pockets the whole tin and ambles off humming happily to himself.

But it is the Iraqi women who are really striking: they are full of ideals, ideas, spunky dreams of a brave new Iraq. The two most important women at the DAC, Ahlam and "Jenny" (an Anglified version of her Arabic name), are totally unalike yet as close as sisters. Ahlam is as plain as an empty plate, a cheerful bucktoothed farmer's wife in modest traditional garb; glamorous Jenny, whose husband is a wealthy Baghdad executive, dresses like an elegant upscale Western businesswoman. Both are fluent in English, and both are outspoken feminists. Under Saddam, Iraqi women enjoyed a level of freedom rare in the Arab world, attending university, working as professors, doctors, scientists, attorneys: couple that with Shi'ism's generally progressive attitude toward women, and their lofty expectations are probably understandable; but I still find them semi-miraculous, especially in the dire realm of present-day Iraq. Jenny's tiny teenaged daughter, Lina, who's in med school though she looks like she is fourteen, tells us she would never marry an Iraqi man: "They are too stupid, and they want to tell you what to do." She wrinkles her nose. "They have lived in the desert so long they have become like camels."

"How about an American man? Would you marry one of them?" Espinosa asks.

"No, I will never marry. Why should I? I want to live my life myself."

Ahlam, Jenny and their female friends at the DAC are tough, independent and not at all shy: they talk to us like human beings, friends. Ahlam is particularly fond of Major Clark, and clucks over his emotional life like a mother hen. It has somehow gotten out that the Major's wife left him before he left for Iraq; when she asks him if perhaps his wife has a boyfriend, evidently he tells her, no, he's sure his wife wouldn't do that. To Ahlam this is sure evidence that the Major doesn't know anything about women.

The DAC women get together and discuss it, and Ahlam goes and asks the Major what he is going to do when he takes his two-week leave from Iraq. He tells her there is a certain woman in England; he met her at a Bank of America conference in London, and he has been calling her regularly since he got to Baghdad. He is going to go to the UK and ask her out to dinner, and then see what happens. And if she says no? Then he'll just spend two weeks in England traveling around by himself before he returns to Baghdad. This confirms the DAC women's opinion that the Major is completely naive and emotionally defenseless, and Ahlam and another young woman named Hanan seek me out when we are at the DAC and ask me if there's anything I or anyone else on the team can do to help Major Clark figure out the female heart and find himself a good woman. I tell them it's beyond me; while I find myself thinking that although the Small Wars Handbook never covered this, surely when the people of an occupied country start worrying about the love life of the soldiers who have come to help them it's got to be a good sign.

For all the emotional intimacy between these women and us, at the same time there's an invisible and indefinable line separating us. Ahlam, Jenny, Hanan and their friends are very, very religious Shi'as, and as such they are virtuous in a sense that we in the West can barely comprehend; not in a prissy, judgmental, holier-than-thou way, but something more relaxed and natural: pure by nature. They are like everybody's sisters. When Espi asks one of the DAC women to explain their seemingly impossible, paradoxical mixture of worldly wisdom and unshakeable virtuousness, she smiles a gnomic smile and says simply, "We are Shi'a girls."

One remarkable thing about these women, at least to me, is their fondness bordering on adulation for Oprah Winfrey. Some satellite channel, probably one of the savvy Beirut operations, beams old Oprah shows across the Middle East every day, and America's wealthiest entertainer has become a superstar to Baghdad's educated Shi'a women. Many of the DAC women watch her religiously, and they quote her opinions and talk admringly of her wisdom. She is the epitiome of all they dream of for themselves: smart, independent, classy, ambitious and benevolent. They know all about her personal life and love the fact that she has never married her boyfriend, Stedman, though they also like her monogamous relationship with him: she is free to live however she wants, but chooses to be virtuous. Perfect!

I have my own set of strange Iraqi experiences when we are out on the streets and crowds gather. Almost inevitably, people start asking if I am a "hajji," an Iraqi, and they refuse to believe my denials. It is mysterious—Cruddas looks a lot more like a local than I do, with his Hispanic features—but it happens time after time. Worse, when I keep denying I am an Iraqi, someone in the crowd usually starts yelling that I am really a *Kuwaiti,* working with the Americans as a mercenary, which is much worse since Iraqis still hate the Kuwaitis, somehow managing to blame them for Saddam's disastrous invasion of their own country, which boomeranged into the Gulf War. No, it doesn't make sense, but then I don't look like an Iraqi, or a Kuwaiti either for that matter.

A whole lot of Iraqi beliefs seem downright crazy by our standards. When U.S. troops first showed up in Iraq, a rumor spread in poor Shi'a neighborhoods that the protective goggles our soldiers wore were really X-ray lenses that could see through clothing; women fled screaming hysterically whenever the lascivious Crusaders showed up. Many Iraqis we talk to also believe there's a secret pipeline carrying Iraqi oil to Israel, giving it away for free, and that our capture of Saddam was a fake, a propaganda stunt: the wild-eyed, disheveled figure we pried out of that spiderhole wasn't really Saddam at all, but an impostor ginned up by the C.I.A. to embarrass and demoralize Iraqis. (Noting the captured Saddam's similarity to an American panhandler, clever GIs here have computer-generated a photo of him with a sign reading WILL GAS KURDS FOR BEER.)

Another popular rumor making the rounds concerns the car bombings that are becoming more and more common in Iraq: the explosions are not the work of Iraqis or Arab terrorists, but really caused by missiles fired from U.S. aircraft, lurking beyond ear- and eyeshot of people on the ground. The Americans hope to trigger distrust and civil war among the Iraqis, to divide and conquer more easily. Most Iraqis view us as magically omnipotent, and believe that nothing happens by accident where we are concerned: there is a secret, malign purpose behind it, aimed at harming Islam.

These kinds of fables are not uniquely Iraqi. When I was living in Pakistan years ago, a locally produced film came out titled *Satanic Verses*. In it, Salman Rushdie was a kind of infidel Dr. No, who ran an anti-Moslem conspiracy from an island somewhere in the Indian Ocean. His secret weapon was his infamous book: he captured faithful Moslems and tortured them to death by playing recordings of the text to them. He was eventually tracked down by two Pakistani commandos and a beautiful Mossad agent who converted to Islam. In the end, a gigantic rotating Koran appeared in the sky and fried Rushdie with laserlike rays of "Allaho akbar." Moslem audiences around the world took the film extremely seriously, and it ended up being the highest grossing movie in the history of Pakistani cinema.

It is not just the uneducated and unsophisticated Iraqis—farmers, street kids, bazaar workmen—who believe these fantastical yarns: *everyone* here does, to one degree or another, including, surprisingly often, sophisticated, intelligent Iraqis like Ajay and al-Janabi. It is almost as if there is a cerebral Unreality Zone, an area of the Iraqi brain that deals with Islam and its enemies. Painful truths are shunted there, where they are erased and replaced by Ali Baba–esque fairy tales with rosy endings.

The most obvious trait of most Iraqis we meet is their extreme *likeability;* they are basically a friendly, curious, instinctively hospitable people. It is significant that after more than a year of American occupation, the great majority of Iraqis are not fighting us; they grumble, they grouse, they complain, but they would never pick up a gun or plant a bomb. The tone of their anti-American rhetoric is more aggrieved than outraged: Why aren't you doing more to help us? Why don't you try and understand us? Why don't you act nicer?

During the period when U.S. forces are besieging the Sadr Brigades in the holy Shi'a cities in the south, the people of al-Khadimiyah, even those who work with CAT-A 13 regularly and have personal friendships with members of the team, are torn in their loyalties. After all, their most sacred shrines are being damaged, and thousands of their fellow Shi'as are being killed. Posters of Moktadar al-Sadr appear everywhere in the neighborhood; they are reportedly printing them up right in the DG's office, where American officers meet with Iraqi officials every day. At one public building, I see an Iraqi National Guard soldier manning a machine gun on the roof, guarding against attacks by the Sadr Brigades; right below him is a big poster of al-Sadr himself, scowling righteously.

But still, the Iraqis' tone remains less angry than hurt. At the height of the tension, the al-Khadimiyah DAC issues a leaflet opposing the American assault on Najaf: it attempts an angry, confrontational tone but keeps backing off into pleas for reason and understanding, all of it undermined by surreal grammar verging on nonsense:

> *In the name of God,*
> *After the favor of God in getting rid of the oppression*
> *and away from aggression and hostility. The neck of*
> *the deprived people look forward to be compensated for*
> *several decades of deprivations hope to live in liberty*
> *and respecting human being better than the previous*

regime. We found that the transitional government used last remedy to solve the crisis by bloody process, as we see the trials of Iraqi forces together with USAF storming by force to enter the holly Nah-jaf [Najaf] city by savage way shedding bloods in total same as the previous regime in opposing up rising during 1991 and the mass graves. We in the same time doom and criticize sharply using restrain against our beloved city holly Najaf, Al-Sader and Shulla cities, and other Iraqi Towns. We warn the transitional government of the continuity in such bloody processes which are against the new system that raise the liberty Flag and democracy.

If this policy started in such way, so what would be the end. We ask the government to the peaceful negotiations and debate to find solution to this crisis in order to make holly Najaf city and return Iraqi citizens dignity.

We call upon our people to solidarity hand in hand to achieve these demands because of the major danger which became useless to arbitrate according to the scattered parties.

God saves Iraq and its people of any badness and leads our people to prosperity and goodness.

Khadimiyah city council

10

WHATEVER ELSE THEY do, a good CAT-A team bonds with the people they work with and forms lasting friendships.

It is certainly happening with the CAT-A 13 troops in al-Khadimiyah; even the irascible Kramer, who professes hatred for pretty much everybody in the world, especially, as he puts it, "goddamn ragheads."

My first real encounter with Kramer came on my second night with the team. Everyone was watching television, and some file footage of the pilgrimage to Mecca came on the screen: hundreds of thousands of Moslems, in a great flowing, enormous swirl around the Ka'aba. I was just about to make some high-flown comment about the amazing power of that place and that faith, drawing millions of people from all over the world, Indonesians, Turks, Afghans, Iraqis and Iranians, black Americans from Detroit and white ones from Marin County, Burmese Rohingyans, Kashmiris, Chinese and Mexicans, like a cosmic magnet, when Kramer beat me to the draw. "Yeah, go ahead and pray to your goddamn Black Stone," he addressed the televised crowd amiably, as if they were his friends. "I'd take me about ten thousand Abrams tanks and form a big circle around that holy city of yours. Then I'd start 'em up, and have 'em all start driving toward the middle till they met. There'd be nothing left but a big ol' pile of turbans and beards and those pointy-toed little slippers y'all like to wear."

I get used to Kramer's fantastically violent soliloquies after a while; he does them in large part to entertain everybody, and it isn't like he is picking on Moslems: he has even worse fates planned for his annoying neighbors back home in Missouri, especially "that big fat old gal next door who lies around in a goddamn bikini all day so I've got to look at her big ugly ass every time I turn around." Even the Summer Olympics, when they come on, draw his ire: "I'd like to take an H-bomb, the biggest one they make, and drop it right in the middle of the Olympic stadium." But since Iraq is where we are, it affords him endless opportunities to focus his destructive imagination on Iraqis, Arabs and Moslems in general.

I suspect he is one of those people who conceal a heart of gold beneath a forbidding exterior, and the proof comes one day when Kramer cooks up barbecued pork for lunch—he is an expert chef, and the team has gotten so spoiled by his cooking that no one has been to the Banzai chow hall for months—and Ajay and al-Janabi drop by unexpectedly, just as Kramer is about to serve up. He takes me aside and whispers frantically, "What do I do? I cooked pork for lunch, and now Ajay and al-Janabi are here."

"Oh, they won't mind. They're cool guys."

"You don't understand. They can't eat pork, and I don't have anything else to offer them." He is genuinelty distressed.

"I think they'll understand. Maybe they can make themselves a sandwich, or grab a snack out of the pantry—or hell, they can just sit here and hang out with us while we eat. Maybe they had lunch on the way here."

But clearly I don't get it: somehow, Kramer is convinced that just being around pork-eaters will hurt Ajay's and al-Janabi's feelings. He hurries off, and the next thing I know he has *hidden* the pot of barbecue and sauce, and is going around buttonholing everyone on the team one by one, whspering to them not to let the two interpreters know what is going on. "But I'm *hungry,*" Cruddas protests plaintively. "I was all set to eat when they showed up."

"Yeah? Well, that's too damned bad. If you go *near* that pork while Ajay and al-Janabi are here, I'll kill you," Kramer informs him.

Oblivious to the drama going on all around them, Ajay and al-Janabi hang around for nearly two hours, conferring with Major Clark, checking out what's on TV, talking to team members about happenings across Iraq. Every time one of them goes near the stove, Kramer runs around fidgeting nervously, or tries to lure them away with clumsy attempts at conversation. "Hey, al-Janabi, ah, what do think that guy, um, that mullah guy, the young one—"

"Moktadar al-Sadr?"

"Yeah, ol' Mookie. Do you think he's gonna keep on causing trouble for us, or is he getting tired of getting his ass whupped?" Through it all, Kramer's teammates are biting their lips to keep from laughing. By the time the interps finally leave, Kramer looks like he has aged another twenty years.

Much of CAT-A 13's success in al-Khadimiyah is due to Colonel Miyamasu, no doubt about it. He's a fascinating character, both bulldog tough and acutely intelligent.

My first encounter with him is at a meeting at the DG's office downtown. Colonel Miyamasu asks al-Doabi (a pseudonym), the shifty DG, why we are continuing to pay the salaries of two hundred municipal truck drivers when there are only twenty vehicles on the al-Khadimiyah books. Al-Doabi smiles his sickly smile and explains that the drivers have threatened to kill him and his assistants if he doesn't keep paying them; most likely he has made a deal with the idle drivers and is splitting their pay with them. But Colonel Miyamasu is having none of it. He interrupts al-Doabi's spiel and says, "Give me the drivers' names, and Colonel Formica and I will round them up and stick them all in Abu Ghraib prison. We'll see how they like that."

Al-Doabi tries to spin his way out of it—he obviously doesn't want to give up his income from the kicked-back salaries: "If you give me time, I'll try to talk to them—" But Colonel Miyamasu cuts him off again in mid-sentence: "No, they're not getting paid anymore unless they're working, and that's that. I'm not using the American taxpayers' money to pay a bunch of bums. And like I said, if they don't like it, we'll see how they like Abu Ghraib Prison.* You can tell them I said so."

Unlike many combat arms officers, Miyamasu is a great supporter of Civil Affairs. He is also the kind of commander who can't abide delays, mediocrity, anything less than 110 percent in efforts and results. A perfect partner for Major Clark, in other words.

The operation Colonel Miyamasu has put together at Banzai FOB is unique in all of Iraq. He has two fluent Arabic-speaking sergeants in his command, and he has stationed them at Banzai's

---

*This was well before the revelations about torture at the prison. Imagine him looking at the situation in Iraq, sticking out that jaw of his, saying "Screw the rules," and charging on full speed ahead to get this damned mixed-up conflict solved, the war won.

north gate, in what they call the Dagger Cell, a combined complaint department, community outreach center and intelligence network. A group of Iraqi regulars, young men and women, hang out there on a permanent basis, and all day people from al-Khadimiyah, the rest of Baghdad and even the Sunni and Shi'a Triangles show up to talk about their problems, ask for assistance and deliver information on terrorist threats and rumors of insurgent attacks. "They tell us they have forward patrol bases where they live, but they're just not the same," one of the sergeants tells me proudly. "They say the word is out across Iraq about Banzai—you can talk to the Americans there, and we'll not only listen, we'll help them out if they're having some problem with the Army or CPA. Some of them have come over a hundred miles just to talk to us."

The whole Cav operation at Banzai is like that: Miyamasu and the officers at the TOC have a hotline set up with the Shi'a elders who run the shrine; whenever they hear about al-Qaeda agents showing up in al-Shula, or some other threat to the neighborhood's peace, the elders call up the Cav and work together to keep things cool.

Several times they have helped circumvent what would have been catastrophic acts: a giant truck bomb that was to crash Banzai's north gate, a demonstration in which snipers and suicide bombers were going to mingle with the crowd of peaceful demonstrators, an RPG assault on a supply convoy, the formation of a joint al-Qaeda–Sadr Brigade cell in a Mehdi Army compound in al-Shula. It is kind of like Neighborhood Watch back home in the States: neighbors watching out for neighbors.

11

EVERYONE IN THE 425th is supposed to get two weeks of home leave sometime during their deployment in Iraq. It is a good thing. Iraq grinds away at you, abrades your strength in countless ways, and it helps to be able to stop and gather yourself together. But as I discover, going home isn't that easy.

At the end of April, I decide I need a break. I get Colonel Lattamore to write up a set of travel orders for me, and I hop a C-130 from BIAP to Kuwait. I go through the bureaucratic mill at Camp Wolverine, change into civilian clothes, take a taxi into Kuwait City and spend a restless night at a budget hotel downtown. I have gotten used to the roar of the cheap team house AC system, and the occasional bang and boom in the night. The hotel is too quiet. The next day I fly to Dubai, spend fourteen hours in transit, and then take a commercial flight to London and across the Atlantic to the USA.

Away from the adrenalized realm of the war, I suddenly realize how bad my body feels. Iraq hammers you with sheer physical abuse: dysentery (what Cruddas likes to call "pissing out your ass"), chronic bronchitis from the dust and smoke, leishmaniasis . . . almost everyone in the 425th has infected sand flea bites that keep on opening up and bleeding months later and trigger symptoms ranging from agonizing itching to edema: your legs swell up with fluid, and your belly bloats till you feel like the Michelin Man. A month ago I caught my left ring finger on a piece of metal as I jumped out of a Humvee, ripping it open and fracturing the bone. I had almost forgotten it all back in Iraq, but now the pain comes crashing back, as if I am coming out of anesthesia. My first night back, I dream a mortar round has gone off, sit up suddenly and somehow smash my face into the wall, breaking my nose. Blood everywhere, and for the next few days I walk around with two black eyes and a schnozz like Cyrano de Bergerac's.

But it's my mind, not my body, that has taken the real hit. I have been looking forward to being home, but now I find I don't really like it; in fact, home doesn't feel like home anymore. When I turn on the news, the war is barely mentioned: there will be a whole raft of reports on celebrity trials, the tribulations of Scott Peterson, Kobe, Michael Jackson and company, and exaltations of the latest box office hit or reality TV shooting star; and only then might they show ten seconds of a burning Humvee, with a casual reference to "two American soldiers killed and three wounded." You would think the war was being fought on Jupiter by a posse of Tongans, for all the interest the media shows. I find that it infuriates me.

Back during the Vietnam War, Professor Leslie Fiedler commented on the divide between the soldiers fighting overseas and the commentators and opinion-makers back home: "[I had] never known a single family that had lost a son in Vietnam, or indeed had one wounded, missing in action or held as a POW; and this despite the fact that American casualties in Vietnam are almost equal to those in World War I. Nor am I alone in this strange plight; in talking to friends about a subject they seem not eager to discuss, I discover they can, must, all say the same."

Well, Iraq is much worse. There is the same class divide, between those who are fighting the war and those whose vocation is to explain what it is all about, but now the explainers aren't even bothering to explain, and no one seems to care. Never has a nation fought a war with so little passion.

And when the Abu Ghraib prison story breaks, it gets even worse: suddenly the American public is looking at the war, only they're not—they are seeing a twisted funhouse mirror image of it. I never met anyone in Iraq who even faintly resembled these trailer trash sadists posing as prison guards. Where are all the good GIs I saw, who visited children's hospitals during their time off, guarded mosques to keep suicide bombers away, were best friends with Iraqi National Guard kids and interpreters? Where are Major Clark, Sergeant Venters, Simms, Frame, Corliss, Baaden?

I think of the Cav soldier I met when the two of us were guarding the DAC during a meeting of local Iraqi civic leaders. He told me we Americans had created the mess in Sadr City: the first Civil Affairs teams stationed there hadn't done nearly enough to help with the problems of overflowing sewage, collapsing roads, a failing electrical system and crime, and the local inhabitants eventually began hating us as much as they had hated Saddam, for the same kinds of reasons. It made him mad: "We have to do better by these people," he said.

He knew all about Sadr City because his wife was over there right now, part of the CA team that took over the neighborhood two months ago, trying to make up for the problems their predecessors had left them. He and his wife never got to see each other: both were on duty full time in separate AOs. They kept in touch by e-mail and phone, and every time fighting broke out in one's area, the other one worried frantically till they heard everything was okay.

Why isn't their story being shown on the air? Why don't the American people get to see Major Clark walking out alone into a hostile crowd to find out what is wrong, or Sergeant Venters distributing fish to his Iraqi workers? It drives me crazy, frustrates and alienates me, makes me so angry I could shoot somebody, if I could figure out who. When people I meet don't want to talk about the war, I despise them: what is there to talk about that is more important, anyway? And when they do want to talk about it, I get just as angry: what makes you think you could ever understand what it is really like over there?

In the end I couldn't wait to get back to Baghdad, and that made me sad. It was as if I had lost something over there, or along the way, a part of myself that I would never find again.

12

AFTER TWO DAYS and nights in Kuwait waiting for a flight and four more days stuck at BIAP, Major Clark and the team pick me up and drive me back to Banzai. When we pull in the compound gate, I feel like I am coming home, back to where I belong.

It's a real Baghdad summer now, 120-plus in the day and lows of maybe 90 at night, zero humidity, and when we get a breeze it's somehow even hotter, like the open door of a blast furnace, tongues of flame licking your face, taking away your very breath, making it hard to inhale. Add armor, Kevlar helmet and the rest, and it's unbelievable. Before he went home on leave, Cruddas had his wife mail him a meat thermometer: one day he stuck it under his body armor for a couple of minutes and came up with 138 degrees.

Al-Janabi tells us the Iraqis think there is air-conditioning built into our armor, another piece of infidels' magic, and that is how we are able to keep running around while the locals are swooning on cots in the shade or holed up indoors with the fan on and the blinds closed. When he told them we aren't wearing portable ACs, he says their estimation of us skyrocketed: "*Wa'Allah,* those crazy Amerikis are *tough!*"

But there is no denying it, the heat just clobbers you, no matter how much you get used to it. By noon you are exhausted; you feel like a 1963 Pinto with a dead battery, and the rest of the day you are running on sheer instinct, plodding along on automatic pilot. Sometimes, like on walking tours of the Taji dump, the world turns into a movie: those are someone else's feet, hitting the hard ground and sending up squirts of white-hot dust, and the contractor's voice seems to come from a million miles away, a message from Betelgeuse: "We now have—completed—new pipe—two more weeks—" I am absolutely amazed, watching the CAT-A 13 people function in this blinding nightmare, adding up numbers, making a cell phone call on the fly to check something out with some office in the Green Zone, jotting a memo, to set up another meeting next week. . . . There are many kinds of heroism, and this determination to keep going, to see every mission through no matter how long it takes, is one of them.

The team has changed in the weeks since I left. Sergeant Goff has left the team; her replacement is a big, cheerful female spec. 4 named Kim Frier, whom the team has nicknamed "Beta": when she transferred in, they put her through a probationary period, testing her out, and Sergeant Paul said it reminded him of beta-testing a computer. At one time or another Beta has been a cowgirl, a homesteader in Alaska, a biker chick, a carny and a bartender; she was living in Florida, working on a community college BA in anthropology and moonlighting as a security guard, when the Army called her up for Iraq. Her first six months in-country she served with CACOM, Civil Affairs Command, chauffeuring officers around the Green Zone; after a lot of kicking and screaming she managed to bail and join CAT-A 13 in the field.

Fat Larry is gone, exiled to the Shi'a Triangle to help beef up the 425th teams down there; he left shortly after I went back to the States. A couple of weeks after he departed, Sergeant Paul intercepted a package sent to Fat Larry from one of his multitudinous girlfriends back home. The package was full of gourmet cookies and sweets, expensive coffee and imported snack foods. Paul carefully replaced each treat with an equivalent item from the PX, the chow hall and MREs, the absolute worst-quality stuff in the world, resealed the package and sent it on to the Fat One. A week or two later Sergeant Paul and Fat Larry were talking on the phone, and Larry began complaining about how stupid his girlfriend was, wasting stamps to send him nearly inedible junk food he could have gotten right here in Iraq. When Sergeant Paul finally broke the news to him, that his package had been shanghaied and his old CAT-A 13 teammates had consumed all the good stuff, he couldn't believe it.

Cruddas is back home on leave, but he will be back in a week and a half.

What is really surprising—unbelievable would be a better word—is that Kramer is still here, especially after I find out his mother died three weeks ago. The Army flew him back to Missouri on compassionate leave, and while he was home he had an Air Force surgeon check out his injured knee. The doctor told him if he returned to active duty in Iraq he had a good chance of suffering permanent damage and never regaining full use of his leg. Despite this, the Army ordered him to report back to Baghdad; they told him that once he was here Army doctors would reevaluate his injury and send him to Germany if he needed fur-

ther treatment. Of course, when Kramer landed at BIAP the supposed reevaluation had vanished off the radar like it was never
there, and he was promptly sent back to CAT-A 13. His injured
knee is still so painful he can barely climb up to man the SAW-
gun, and the Cav docs at Banzai are dosing him with codeine,
Percocet and Vicodin just to keep him semi-ambulatory. Between missions he limps around with a cane.

It's really great to see the gnarly old ex-Marine again, but I
wish he wasn't here; he's done his duty a hundred times over and
then some, and he should be back home with his wife and children for good, while he can still walk. It's all so unnecessary, unjust and mean-spirited that it's actually surreal: the Army works
in wondrous ways, its blunders to perform.

I quickly catch up on how things are going in al-
Khadimiyah; predictably, there is good news and bad news.

In the bad news department, al-Shula's sewer problem still
hasn't been solved. After the team found the pump trucks at the
water treatment plant, they informed the al-Khadimiyah civil au
thorities, but it took the Iraqis over a month to send drivers to re-
trieve them. Then it took several more weeks to get the trucks
out in the streets, working. And *then* they never seem to work in
al-Shula, though it has by far the worst problem with overflowing sewage. Al-Doabi, the shifty-looking little city manager who
operates out of the DG office in the heart of al-Khadimiyah,
keeps coming up with excuses, but it is clear we are seeing the
same old story: no one likes the people in al-Shula; they are
poor, slum dwellers, and many of them are recent immigrants
from outside Baghdad, so no one wants to help them. As

Sergeant Paul frequently points out, the Iraqis are radical IM-
BYs: if something good is going to happen they want it in their
backyard and nowhere else. It is a classic case of what an En-
glishman referred to as "the life of high crime that passes for politics in the East." More weeks have gone by, and the situation is
growing markedly worse as the raw effluents cook in the summer
heat; kids in al-Shula get sick, infected with nameless diseases
carried by flies breeding and feeding in and on the mess. Major
Clark calls al-Doabi repeatedly, trying to get the trucks over to
al-Shula, but the DG's reply is always the same: not to worry, he
has fifteen trucks at his disposal, ten old ones and the five we
found, and it's only a matter of time before they get around to
the mess in al-Shula.

A week after my return, the Major is having another of his
endless meetings in al-Doabi's office. The air-conditioning is on
the schnitz, the room feels like a pizza oven, and every few seconds someone gets a call on their cell phone and begins a long
conversation that totally disrupts the proceedings; this despite a
sign on the wall that warns, NO SELL PHONE CALLS. Finally Major
Clark manages to ask al-Doabi how many pump trucks he has on
hand; the little man gets out a tiny notebook, consults it and
looks up with a smile: "Three," he says.

There's a moment of shocked silence in the room, as Major
Clark looks at Sergeant Paul, who looks at Grundman. "*Three?*"
Major Clark asks. "You had fifteen last week."

"Did I say three? I meant thirteen," al-Doabi says hurriedly.

"You had fifteen last week. What happened to the other two?"

"Ah, you see, they disappeared."

"Disappeared?"

"Yes, the trucks, and the drivers, too. But I'm sure there is no problem. Both the drivers are good men. I know both of them, and their families."

"The two trucks—they're both the new ones, right?" Major Clark asks, already knowing the answer.

"Yes, yes, the new ones. But the drivers, they are good men. They will bring the trucks back."

It turns out the "good men" have buggered off to Jordan and sold the trucks there. No one knows who ultimately shared in the profits, but I suspect that some portion is lining the pockets of corrupt officials. Over the next month or so more pump trucks vanish the same way. Eventually al-Doabi gets sacked, and replaced by an actual trained urban administrator. Maybe, just maybe, al-Shula will finally get its long-promised cleanup.

Meanwhile there are other fiascos and FUBARS. One of CAT-A 13's biggest accomplishments has been establishing a huge sanitary landfill and recycling center out in southern Taji, where trash and refuse from all over western Baghdad can be safely disposed of. The contractor did a great job, building berms around the site to contain it, digging out separate areas to sort and recycle glass, plastic, metal, construction material and so on. He even put in a concrete pad and a high-pressure hose line so trucks can be cleaned before they leave the site; outside the main gate he planted a lawn and ornamental shrubs, and every time we go by there is a sprinkler spinning away, watering the new vegetation.

But as soon as the dump is up and running, neighboring Iraqis begin shooting at the contractor's employees, and every few days he receives death threats. It turns out the landfill site is next to an abandoned factory complex owned by "E-Z Electric," a gang of Saddam-era businessmen who claim the dump is on "their" land. They demand that Major Clark shut down the landfill immediately.

Instead of sending Colonel Miyamasu's troops to arrest these characters, Clark meets with them at the E-Z Electric offices in the factory compound. I have never seen a sleazier collection of reptiles in my life: oily, sly-looking men in cheap suits and fake designer watches. One looks like an iguana, another like a snapping turtle, a third like a fruit bat. Despite the fact that the factory buildings are gutted and the only employees in sight are fewer than a dozen goons loitering around doing nothing, they claim the new landfill is interfering with their thriving industrial operation. To try to prove their point, they produce a collection of blatantly specious "business documents," not one of which offers any kind of proof E-Z Electric has ever manufactured as much as a forty-watt lightbulb. There are import licenses for everything from pharmaceuticals and toys to kitchenware and appliances, but as Major Clark points out to them, they don't need a factory to bring foreign goods into Iraq: manufacturing and importing are like apples and oranges. There are also hilarious bogus letters purporting to be from big-time business executives in Western Europe who want to partner with E-Z Electric: they are printed on cheap stationery that looks like Third World toilet paper, half the words are misspelled, and the very names of the corporations are on the order of Trans-Global International Enterprises Holdings Ltd. and Amalgamated Unlimited United Hemispheric Industries and Trading. Resisting the urge to frogmarch these crooks out the door at gunpoint and transport them to Abu Ghraib, Major Clark politely warns them to stop harassing the landfill contractor, and tells them he will check their claims with the Baghdad city government.

In the end, it turns out E-Z Electric has no right to the land-fill site at all, of course. And the Major finds a way of solving the shooting problem: he has the contractor hire the people doing the shooting as workers.

And then there is the Baghdad Gate contractor. He has done a great job—restoring the antique tile work on the gate, installing modern rest rooms in the base, putting in a park and playground next to it—so much so that Major Clark recommends he be hired for several more public works projects. The problem is, all this draws the attention of the local criminals who prey on successful Iraqis, and a gang of them kidnaps the contractor and holds him for ransom. His family ends up buying him back for $50,000, a fortune in today's Iraq, but while he is held captive he is beaten up and tortured. When we go to see him after his release, he is preparing to take his family on an extended holiday outside Iraq. What is really depressing is who kidnapped him: while he was being held, tied up and blindfolded, he recognized the voices of several local policemen. When the Major offers to turn the infor-mation over to the local government so they can apprehend the guilty cops, the contractor waves him off: "There's nothing you can do," he says. "Everyone in Iraq is crooked. I will take care of it myself." Presumably that means he will hire his own muscle, or call up some heavies from his extended family, clan or tribe, and exact his own private payback. But it's yet another example of the difficulties facing those who want to improve life in Iraq, problems the authors of the Small Wars Manual never imagined.

In the same vein is the crazed brouhaha over the new bar-racks room for the guards at the al-Khadimiyah equipment yard.

Like the DAC, this is another of the neighborhood's nerve centers, where American money meets the local power structure, producing a constant flow of deals, jobs, partnerships, alliances and scams. There are always dozens of drivers, equipment operators, mechanics, foremen and laborers bustling around, as well as friends, relatives, salesmen, peddlers and hangers-on.

The contractor did a good job on the new building for the guards: there is space for them to sleep, a little kitchen and a toilet in a small adjacent structure. In fact, he did too good a job: it looks so nice that the manager of the equipment yard wants to leave his old cottage next to the gate and take it over. He is really being childish: the cottage is actually beautiful, sturdy and comfortable looking, with flowers growing over the porch out front. But the manager insists that new equals better and since he is, after all, the Manager, he should have a better place than the guards who work for him.

One of Major Clark's strongest suits is his willingness to work on Iraqi Time. Iraqis like to make things like meetings last as long as possible, stretching them out with plenty of tea, casual gossip, interruptions for chats on the phone, and so on. To be efficient American-style borders on being rude. Either deliberately or subconsciously, Major Clark has "gone Iraqi." He will leave a meeting at the DAC and then stand outside, yakking away with the Iraqis, endlessly; it drives the rest of the team crazy, but the Iraqis love it. "Your Major Clark, he is exactly like us," one of the DAC members once told me. So instead of telling the manager sorry, what's done is done and that's that, the Major starts negotiating with the manager and the guards, trying to find a compromise.

It really is funny, though no one on the team thinks so at the time. It is a typical—meaning awful—summer day, 120, 125 in the shade, and there is no shade. The CAT-A 13 troops are in the two Humvees, waiting to go home to Banzai. There have already been several missions, with visits to the DAC, the Taji dump, the decrepit sewage pumping station in al-Hurriyah, etcetera, etcetera, ad infinitum. And now they wait, and wait, and keep on waiting, as Major Clark, with Sergeant Paul and the team's translator in tow, embarks on what is literally "shuttle diplomacy," walking back and forth between the cottage and the new guardhouse, along with the opposing parties, debating the issue.

An hour and change goes by, with more than ten round trips between the two buildings: Grundman starts out counting, but gives up after a while. The heat is unbelievable, especially for people wearing body armor and Kevlar helmets. The ice in the coolers has long since melted, and the last bottles of drinking water are as hot as soup, undrinkable. The metal on the Humvees is too hot to touch. Grundman and Kramer, the two SAW-gunners, look comatose, slumped at their weapons. Beta, sitting behind the wheel of her Humvee, stares straight ahead like a zombie. Espinosa looks like her mind is on a beach at Laguna.

Finally the dilemma is solved. With Solomonic wisdom, the Major convinces the manager that his cottage is just fine for the time being, and meanwhile CAT-A 13 will put in for emergency funds to have a new manager's residence built, bigger and better than the guardhouse. For their part, the guards are smugly pleased: they get to keep their nice new hooch. The Major explains it all to us when he returns to the Humvees with Sergeant Paul and Ayat. Kramer's comment seems to speak for everyone: "Like a bunch of motherfucking kids. Ain't none of them worth a pound of piss."

And then Major Clark breaks the news: there is just enough daylight left to drive up to al-Shula and do a quick survey of the sewage pumping substations there.

*   *   *

Meanwhile the fighting is still going on unabated. My journal records at least one incident every twenty-four hours, usually as many as a half dozen. On July 14, around ten A.M., there is a mortar barrage, and an hour later, when I am over at the Moonlight Café e-mailing, another round hits just outside. Around dusk there is another barrage, along with what sounds like a small arms firefight over by the main gate, and late that night more mortar rounds. A day or two later we are driving in the main gate after a day in the field when a Cav sergeant runs up to us and yells, "Go, go, go! They're gonna hit us with RPGs!" Evidently the Shi'as from the mosque have called up, warning we are about to be attacked. We speed out of there, back to the team house. The attack never comes off, probably because the gate guards were on full alert, but that night there are a lot of mortar rounds and what sound like the big Brazilian rockets the insurgents have been importing.

One of the most dangerous areas on the FOB is the stretch of road between the team house and the Moonlight, about two hundred yards to the south. More than once I have gone over to the Moonlight to e-mail, heard a couple of mortar rounds hit nearby while I am online, and while walking home I have noticed a new crater or two in the pavement, right on my footsteps.

The trouble is everywhere, omnipresent. One day when we are leaving the Green Zone we pass the heavily guarded convoy of the Iraqi justice minister; the next day we learn that a suicide car bomber hit two or three minutes after we passed, killing six of the minister's bodyguards and just missing him.

An Army officer is discovered in the Green Zone at two in the morning with his throat cut; the stories are murky, but sup-

posedly he survives and is flown back to the States. Green Zone
residents begin carrying loaded weapons, and the zone's busy
nightlife slows to almost nothing as people stay at home behind
locked doors after dark,

A GI is snatched by terrorists right in the heart of Camp Victory. A couple of hajji workers call him over to help them start
their stalled car; when he leans over to look under the hood they
club him in the head, stuff his unconscious body in the trunk and
smuggle him off the post. The soldier awakens some time later,
kicks the trunk open and jumps out of the speeding vehicle. Fortunately he isn't badly hurt when he hits the asphalt, and on top
of that he is in a more or less friendly neighborhood; somebody
hails an American patrol, and he is returned to Camp Victory
safely. An intel report says that al-Qaeda terrorists are offering
$100,000 for the capture of a female American soldier; they plan
to behead her on television. Sergeant Major Abarca, the tall,
hard-as-nails SF soldier on loan to the 425th, discovers an
al-Qaeda training film being shown on the Internet. It consists of
a rough videotape of the car bombing of a Russian convoy in
Chechnya, shown without commentary, just ambient sound. In
the video, insurgents pack the trunk of an old sedan with rockets
and RPG rounds, wired up to explode by remote control. The
car is left by the side of the road, against a wall. The rest is shot
from a couple of hundred feet away, from the vantage point of the
concealed bombers. A lookout waves and shouts, and then comes
running and hides next to the cameraman. A few seconds later a
truck column drives into view. When the center of the convoy is
passing by the parked car, there is a huge explosion, and the
trucks vanish in fire, smoke and shattered flesh and metal.

Predictably, it's not long before the Iraqi insurgents start using car bombs in addition to IEDs. They have several obvious advantages. First, you can pack a lot of explosives into a vehicle, and on top of that the gas in the tank intensifies the blast. The car itself is a great source of shrapnel: thousands of pounds of scrap metal and shattered glass, slicing up everyone and everything in the area. And a VIED, Vehicular Improvised Explosive Device, is mobile: you can drive it to the point of attack and leave it, or, in an increasingly popular technique, a suicidal driver can swerve the rolling bomb into the middle of an American convoy or crash it into a car carrying an important Interim Government official, and then set it off. It is almost impossible to defend against these freeway kamikazes.

The best antidote for fear is humor, mockery, and Kramer keeps everyone's spirits up with his contemptous commentaries on the enemy's military prowess, or lack thereof. One night in the TV room, he tells us about a film that he saw somewhere, shot by the insurgents, of one of their operations in Baghdad. "This one dumb son of a bitch sneaks up to a corner, sticks his AK-47 around the side of the building and fires a whole clip without even looking. Then he goes to the back of the line to get another clip of ammo from some old son of a bitch who has a bucket full of ammo, and meanwhile another dumb SOB goes to the corner and shoots without looking, same as the last one. There's a whole row of these guys, and none of them know what the hell they're shooting at."

He has everyone laughing so hard they can't stop. He continues: "Then they showed one of their mortar crews. The dumb SOB in charge sights it by lying on the ground and staring up the length of the tube into the fucking *sky*! They fire it, and their observer standing up on this dirt pile waves his arms and cheers. So they drop another round in and it goes off, and now the guy on the dirt pile looks real disappointed, like he can't understand why the first one hit the target and the second one didn't. Well, shit, the dumb motherfuckers didn't have the base plate anchored, and the whole damn mortar moved about two feet from the recoil when they fired it the first time."

A minute later, as if on cue, the TV shows an insurgent mortar crew over in east Baghdad: they fire off a round, and the whole mortar mount just collapses, disintegrates, and the mortar collapses in the dirt. The timing is exquisite, too perfect. You can hear Cruddas's high-pitched peals of laughter miles away across the Tigris.

One night we hear the heaviest close-in fighting yet: just off to the west, the angry sputter of countless AK-47s firing away on full auto and two machine guns, 12.7s, dueling it out. Major Clark, Sergeant Paul, Beta and I stand outside watching as twin arcs of tracer crisscross, one firing north and the other counter-firing south. They're shooting right in downtown western al-Khadimiyah, in the crowded neighborhoods beyond the shrine. The Major and Sergeant Paul go in to check on the fighting over the radio with the 1/5 Cav TOC, and Sergeant Paul reappears a couple of minutes later along with Grundman, Kramer and Cruddas, shaking his head and laughing. "Fucking Iraqis," he says.

"What?"

"All that fucking gunfire? It's two police stations, the one in al-Shula and the one in al-Hurriyah, shooting at each other. The guys in Hurriyah got shot at from the north, and they fired back with their heavy machine gun and hit the al-Shula police station by mistake. The al-Shula cops thought the Sadr Brigades were attacking them again, so they started shooting back. Now the cops are going at it on both sides with everything they've got. Colonel Miyamasu keeps radioing them, telling them to cease fire, but they won't listen—each one wants the other to stop shooting first."

We're all laughing, watching the gunfire arc back and forth, solid streams slowing to dit-dot-dits of flying sparks, then picking up again—hundreds, thousands of big incandesecent slugs raining on the city.

"Maybe the silly fuckers'll kill each other," Kramer says.

"Are you kidding?" Grundman scoffs. "They could shoot at each other all night long and they'd never hit each other."

"I feel sorry for the poor people who live around those guys," Cruddas says.

"Yeah—'Let' s get a house next to the police station, dear, it'll be safe.' "

"Yeah, right—'Oh shit, I hear gunshots, better call the cops.' "

"Whoops, it *is* the cops. *Now* what the fuck?!?"

"Better call the Sadr Brigades and ask them to kill the cops."

"Let 'em kill each other off. You know, Iraq wouldn't be such a bad place if it wasn't for all these fucking Iraqis."

We watch the red fire continue to rain down. "They're going to burn out the barrels on those guns," Sergeant Paul observes.

"We'll just buy 'em new ones," says Kramer.

"This is really pathetic," Beta says.

There is more sorrow than scorn behind our laughter: *Poor old Iraq.*

13

Colonel Miyamasu once told me, "If I could just give Major Clark ten milllion dollars with no strings attached, our whole job here would get done. If we could clone twenty or thirty of him, the war would be over." He isn't exaggerating by much.

One evening Major Clark calls the team together and announces, "Since we're shorthanded, I'm going to start rolling with the INGs. Starting tomorrow, we're taking two of them with us every day." The INGs are the Iraqi National Guard troops the 1/5 Cav have been training at Banzai over the past few months. Many of them are young Shi'a women, not much taller than their AK-47s, who tell us they enlisted to defend their country against foreign terrorists and fundamentalists who want to take away their rights as women. What they lack in experience they more than make up for in fervor: I see one girl soldier actually weeping after she got a less than perfect score firing up targets with her AK-47. We often see the INGs doing PT before dawn, running laps around Banzai; the men are like recruits everywhere, they lollygag and laugh their way along in creeper gear, but the women run like the wind, dead serious, like they are running for their lives.

For a moment no one on the team reacts to the Major's announcement, and then Sergeant Paul speaks up: "Is this a brigade-level command, sir? Or did it come down from the Cav, or battalion?"

"None of the above," Major Clark says. "It's my idea. I've been thinking about it for a while, and I finally took it to Colonel Miyamasu and he okayed it. He thinks it'll be good for the INGs and for us—it'll help us deal with the Iraqi people, having them along. Anyhow, it's their country, so why shouldn't they go out and fight for it?" That's that: once again CAT-A 13, led by Major Clark, is breaking new ground.

Predictably, the team members grouse and complain about the new plan. "As soon as trouble starts, I'm shooting the fucking INGs first," Kramer says. "I don't trust any of 'em." But the next day, when the first pair of gawky, nervous-looking recruits shows up, everything goes smoothly. Both the INGs are men, and one speaks English fluently; they are both so eager to do well it is impossible not to like them. The English speaker, named Zien, quickly bonds with Cruddas: it turns out he has a black belt in Tae Kwon Do, one of Cruddas's enthusiasms, and the two are soon debating who is the more authentic, Steven Seagal, Bruce Lee or Jackie Chan. Midway through the blazing hot day the younger ING gets out a bottle of cloudy-looking water and prepares to drink; Kramer, who had proclaimed he wouldn't share his food or water with "those ING motherfuckers," fishes a bottle of ice water out of the cooler and hands it to the kid. He takes the bottle of dirty water and tosses it out of the Humvee. "You don't want to drink that shit," he tells the recruit. "They probably got it right out of the fucking river. If you want water, drink the stuff in the cooler."

If there's a problem with the INGs, it's that they are almost too serious about their job. Both of them are in the back of the second Humvee, and as we weave through the traffic they point their weapons at any drivers who don't get out of the way fast enough, cursing in Arabic and shouting bloodcurdling threats. Any Iraqi who talks backs gets a raised middle finger from Zien, and an AK-47 pointed right at him to drive the point home. Major Clark has to counsel the two INGs to be more polite to their countrymen: "We want you to help us make friends here, not start a new war." He grins.

Over the next weeks we get used to working alongside the Iraqis, and I can't help but notice the positive reaction they get from the civilian population. Kids point and cheer, motorists honk and give the thumbs-up: you can tell Iraqis, at least in our predominantly Shi'a neighborhoods, are excited and proud to see their countrymen patrolling the streets. If we are ever going to succeed here, this is a vital part of it.

Major Clark tells me that about the same time he came up with the idea of the INGs he asked the higher-ups at Camp Victory if he could start flying Iraqi flags on the Humvees when out in the field. That was way, way too radical for the Big Army, of course, and I'm sure the Major never really expected to get it approved. But as he says, "This is Iraq, and from what I'm told we didn't conquer the country, we came here to liberate it and then hand it back over to the people. So why not fly their flag?"

CAT-A 13 starts pulling medcaps, mobile walk-in clinics, with docs from the 1/5 Cav. It works like this: the Major meets with people in the neighborhoods and ascertains there's a need for free medical care, he finds a good location, and sets a date. The Psy Ops guys send out sound trucks informing the locals;

and then on the appointed morning the Cav goes out along with the CAT-A 13, sets up shop and begins treating patients. They usually bring along a couple of Abrams tanks, a few Bradleys and a bunch of armed Humvees for protection: any big gathering like a medcap is a target for terrorists, and we don't want our Iraqi friends to come in for medical treatment and get blown to bits by a suicide bomber. INGs also help provide security: it is a big morale booster for the Iraqis, to see troops from their own armed forces side by side with American soldiers, keeping the peace.

The first medcap is held in an empty compound that was once part of a women's prison, close to the al-Khadimiyah maintenance yard. When we arrive to set up, patients are already beginning to line up outside the gate, men and women in separate queues. It is just an impression, but most of the men look pretty healthy: you get the feeling many of them have shown up out of curiosity, or because they don't have anything better to do. Old gaffers in robes chat together in line, checking out the American women soldiers and gawking at female INGs toting AK-47s nearly as big as they are. In the other line are women with sick, dull-eyed babies and small children flushed with fever. The docs take the women and children first.

It is a blazing hot day, and the CAT-A 13 troops keep busy bringing water to the people waiting in line and helping control the crowds. We know the folks in this area really well. Beta has a new playground under construction right next to the medcap site, and both she and Espi are bona-fide celebrities among the neighborhood kids: at least a half dozen of the tiny boys have proposed marriage to them. This familiarity helps keep things under control. We hand out toys, baseball caps and Iraqi flags. The temperature reaches 120-plus. It's hard, exhausting work, but well worth it. By the end of the day the docs have treated 175 patients.

Taji, and yet another medcap, in the Neighborhood Advisory Council compound there. This is a bad 'hood—its rural precincts stretch way northward to what I think of as the Little Sunni Triangle—Baquba, Balat, Sammara—but today's mission goes smoothly. CAT-A 13 acts as kind of a crowd control decoy, parking away from the compound gate and drawing people around us and away from the medcap itself. They toss out soccer balls, toys and candy, while inside the compound Ayat and al-Janabi help translate for the Cav doctors. About midway through the hot, dusty day, a kid runs past the gate yelling "Kill Americans! Kill Americans!" I suspect someone put him up to it, taught him to memorize the words, and most likely he has no idea of what they mean—"Hey, if you shout 'Kill A-me-ri-cans' four times they'll give you a thousand dinars"—but the other locals don't like it at all. The other kids grab him and beat the hell out of him, till the Cav soldiers rescue him. Two minutes later the boy's father shows up and he starts to wail on the poor little guy, and again the Cav troops have to intervene. Finally the local sheikh shows up with a big stick and the kid gets whacked again, till the Cav calls the old guy off. The boy spends the rest of the day glued to the Cav sentries at the gate, who console him with sweets and a Black Knights baseball cap.

*   *   *

The Cav docs consult with Major Clark, and they decide ro do a medcap over in al-Shula. That area is as dangerous as ever: IEDs show up almost every day along Route Tampa, the main military route that runs from Abu Ghraib to Taji, and Army patrols get shot at regularly. Just the other day a soldier was killed by a gunman right in front of al-Shula's central police station. That makes it all the more important that the Cav and CAT-A 13 try to do a medcap there, to show the locals they still want to help them.

Major Clark ends up picking a site for the medcap in a school on a busy street corner south of Tampa; the heavy traffic passing by makes it vulnerable to a drive-by shooting or suicide car bomb, but the school is located in the middle of a densely populated lower-class neighborhood with a lot of inhabitants in need of free medical care.

Early on the day of the medcap CAT-A 13 sets up in the vacant lot in front of the school. People begin showing up in droves; one man is so shriveled up and wasted from what is probably MS that Grundman and one of the Cav troops end up half-carrying him into the school. A couple of INGs from Banzai are manning a machine-gun position on the roof, watching for Bad Guys. Just below them on the wall the school's headmistress has plastered a big poster of Moktadar al-Sadr, in an attempt to safeguard the place from possible attackers. Iraq is a complex place, and Iraqis do whatever they have to do to get by.

Grundman has just found an unexploded RPG warhead half-hidden under some trash in the vacant lot; we carefully move it off to one side, away from the school, and are debating whether or not to call the Combat Engineers' UXO squad when a car comes squealing up and a couple of young Iraqis jump out. They've just found an IED, a booby-trapped mortar round, in the front yard of a friendly sheikh just off Route Tampa. The sheikh lives on a block of row houses crowded with families, and they don't know what to do; they've been trying to clear the street of people, but no one will listen to them. If the IED goes off, a lot of people will be killed and injured.

The team grabs Ajay and al-Janabi from inside the school— the Cav have their own interpreters—and they saddle up and follow the young Iraqis to the sheikh's house. Several Iraqi cops have arrived on the scene and are milling around ineffectually. Major Clark, Sergeant Paul and I walk over and check out the IED, followed by the cops. A black plastic bag nestles in the corner of the yard by the front gate; looking closer, you can see the stubby 60mm mortar shell inside, wrapped in red and yellow wire. You can't tell if it is designed to be triggered by remote control, or if was set to explode if someone moves it. Major Clark, who occasionally errs on the side of boldness, pokes at it with the muzzle of his M-16, and the cops scatter. Sergeant Paul and I quietly suggest that touching the IED might not be a good idea, and the Major grins, nods and backs off.

The sheikh is already long gone, but there are still hundreds of people on the block, in the street. With the help of the police we get the neighbors on both sides to move out, and then we cordon off the whole end of the block. Groups of kids keep trying to get past us to look at the bomb—schools are out in Iraq for the summer—and we are continually shepherding them away. There is a big crowd on the corner where the side street meets Route Tampa, and everyone seems happy that we are there keeping an eye on the children. A shopkeeper even brings us soft drinks.

It takes over an hour for the bomb squad to arrive, and when they do they take one look at the IED and bolt back to their armored van, yelling to us to move back another twenty meters; we have been standing way too close, well within the IED's blast radius. When we leave, they unpack one of their ingenious little remote-controlled mini-tractors and guide it toward the bomb. The tractor is equipped with a video camera and an array of tools to defuse the device safely.

A couple of minutes later the team is back at the medcap. More Iraqis are showing up for treatment, and the lines are still long. CAT-A 13 still has four or five hours to go before quitting time, and then Major Clark wants to check out a new report of broken sewer lines up in the dire slums of northwest al-Shula. It's all in a day's work.

14

Sometimes it seems like the official CA uniform should be a BOHICA ("Bend Over Here It Comes Again") baseball cap from the brigade quartermaster, a set of red woolen Arctic long johns and two left desert boots, one XL and the other XS. Sergeant Paul has a cap with snivel affairs embroidered across the front; that would work well, too.

This is supposed to be the greatest, most modern army in the world, but the CA troops definitely have problems with some of their most basic gear. Commo, for instance: the 425th's radios are hard to program and, worse, they tend to conk out in the field. Grundman spends hours tinkering with them, coaxing them to work. Sometimes CAT-A 13 is convoying down the road and they are reduced to signaling each other with hand gestures and trying to shout loud enough to be heard.

The cell phone situation is another disgrace. Supposedly a Kuwaiti company with an immaculate record of service and maintenance originally got the phone contract for U.S. forces in Iraq, only to be bumped by a certain big American phone company that recently flirted with chapter 11 and needed rescuing. At first the U.S. company provided pretty good service, but by mid-summer, at least within the 425th, the service has become dismal. When people get calls on one of these crap gadgets, their best move is to find out who is calling and their callback number in the first twenty seconds; then, when the phone does its usual trick of chopping up the conversation into unintelligible bleeps and blats, they can then hang up and call their party back on an Iraqi cell phone that actually works. Major Clark makes a special trip to the phone company office in the Green Zone to try to get our cell phone service fixed, only to find the door locked, no lights on inside, and a sign informing him that the company no longer provides repairs or services its own products! There is also a number you can call for further information when the office is closed, but when the Major dials it, using his Iraqi cell phone of course, he hears the phone inside the deserted office ringing over and over and over again, till he takes the hint and gives up.

The team's vehicles are another source of constant grief. When I flew through Kuwait on my initial journey to Baghdad, there were hundreds of beautiful brand-new armored Humvees lined up next to the tarmac; they were still sitting there when I flew through on my way to and from the States in June. Meanwhile CAT-A 13, along with scores of other Army units in Iraq, is making do with antiquated open-backed armorless Hummers. If we had had the new ones, Kramer most likely would have escaped the IED attack unscathed, his lower body inside the vehicle's armored interior, his upper body protected by a built-in bulletproof shield. Some desperate GIs have paid Iraqi welders to fit improvised steel plating on the outsides of their Hummers, but Major Clark says the solution is worse than the problem: the funky Iraqi armor looks sturdy enough, but it's made of the wrong kind of steel, not the high-tech ballistic variety, and a hit from an RPG or a heavy enough bullet would shatter the stuff, producing even more razor-sharp shrapnel to cripple, maim and kill.

Finally, after six months in-country, CAT-A 13 receives two of the new improved Humvees, armor-plated, with ballistic windshields and windows that can stop an AK-47 round, and air-conditioning. For several days they roll around in style, and then the inevitable snafu strikes like a sand asp: it turns out the new Humvees are registered on the books of one of the other 425th teams, and even though the other guys aren't using them they want them back: bookkeeping and regulations. We drive them back to BIAP, leave them sitting in the A-LOC parking lot where they will no doubt remain for eternity, and in their place we get two newly armored Humvees that are, in a word, lemons. Everything on them goes wrong—electrical system, oil pressure, turn signals, suspension—plus one of them is both dramatically underpowered and overheats when driven above 45 mph. The team wastes precious days with one or both vehicles in the repair shop at the Banzai motor pool, only to have them bonk again as soon as they roll out. Once or twice the radiator on the worse of the clunkers boils over when the team is in no-man's-land, stranding us in strange neighborhoods we don't know, leaving us standing around on the side of the road waiting for the damn thing to cool down. It's a miracle some Bad Guy doesn't drive by, check the team out and return to blow us away.

Even the indefatigable Major Clark sometimes runs short of optimism. A few days ago he told me, "The Iraqis don't listen to me anymore. The DAC has more funding than the 1/5 Cav now, and I guess it's all about the money. It makes me wonder what I'm doing here. I guess I'll just keep on working till it's time to leave. Then the Army'll send me back here next year, or someplace else, maybe Afghanistan. They'll probably send new people here, who have to learn everything all over again—that's how they seem to like to do things." He pauses. "You know, before I told you I was thinking of signing up for another tour right away, especially if they could guarantee me an assignment back here in al-Khadimiyah. Of course, they told me they couldn't or wouldn't do that—'You'll go where we send you.' Now I'm not even sure I want to stay in the Army. I think I could do more with a civilian aid group, an NGO. The way the Army does things just wastes so much time."

Over the past weeks Colonel Miyamasu and the 1/5 have left Banzai and are stationed down around Najaf; they are the Quick Reaction Force for all of Iraq, and are needed there to help defeat the Sadr Brigades and drive them out of the holy city. Banzai is now manned by a skeleton force, a hodgepodge of troops from headquarters companies, Combat Engineering companies, and so on.

This has triggered yet another piece of absurdity, one that is making CAT-A 13's mission in al-Khadimiyah even harder. All of the combat arms units temporarily assigned here already have their own CA teams opconned to them; instead of plugging into CAT-A 13, which knows the area better than anyone, they are insisting on having "their" Civil Affairs teams move in and take over: it'll look better on their commanders' records when they leave Iraq, and it's probably easier on the copy machine commandos who do bookkeeping and paperwork at BIAP and the Green Zone.

Anyhow, the team suddenly finds itself barred from much of its AO, its missions suspended, frozen in place, at this most critical of times. The 425th isn't going to be here in Iraq that much longer, a huge amount of work remains to be finished, and now Major Clark and the team have to sit on their hands and watch as time runs out on project after project. Of course when the 1/5 returns from Najaf and Banzai's temporary tenants return to their old AOs, the CA troops they brought here with them will be gone, too. What kind of effective CA work are they going to accomplish during their brief stay here?

Someone here once summed up the CA effort in Iraq as "the right people in the wrong place at the wrong time doing the right thing." In recent weeks, Sergeant Paul has begun referring to it as, "Reinventing the flat tire."

All of this weighs heavily on Major Clark. He bombards USAID in the Green Zone with requests for additional funding, and spends long nights at the Moonlight e-mailing NGOs all over the world, seeing if he can get them to pitch in. He is down to two or three hours of sleep a night now, and he doesn't even take time to eat. One night, when Kramer has concocted a gourmet Thai noodle dish out of mess hall beef, French dressing, trail mix, spices and Iraqi pasta, the Major sticks his head in the door of the TV room where everyone is eating and announces that he is off to the Moonlight to research aquaculture and solar power funding and he doesn't know when he'll be back. As he goes out the door, he is shoveling cold ravioli straight from the can with a plastic spoon, his first and only meal of the day. He was always skinny, but now he is beginning to look downright ethereal, wraithlike.

I don't tell him, but I think at least some of Major Clark's depression is really because he and the team have done so much here that they are working themselves out of a job. It's the same kind of feeling a mother has when she sends her son off for his first day of school. The boy is smiling and self-confident, and the woman finds herself wishing he wasn't; that she hadn't raised him to be so strong so fast.

In her own quiet, self-effacing way Beta ends up doing miracles with the women's projects she is in charge of helping. She is squeezing four or five thousand out of the Army budget for the women's center at the DAC, enough to renovate a whole building for the center and set up computer and arts and crafts classes, lectures on how women can start small businesses, and political action committees to encourage both women and men to take part in local and national politics. These DAC women are incredibly dedicated and courageous, Iraqi Joans d'Arc, the stuff of legends. A couple of them are working in the Sunni area of Taji, risking their lives to build democracy among fundamentalists and Ba'ath Party stalwarts who threaten to kill them if they persist; they keep on pushing, even when an Iraqi man doing a similar job is murdered and their homes and offices are bombed.

Good old Beta. Working with Iraqi women is more than a job to her; it is a passion, a vocation felt deep inside. Years ago she was the victim of an abusive relationship that ended when she was nearly beaten to death by her psychopathic boyfriend, and you can tell she is determined to free her Iraqi sisters from the threat of that kind of violence and suppression. Up until recently the DAC women's group has been under the thumb of a malignant hydrant-shaped gorgon named Fatimah. Fatimah was reportedly a kind of junior neighborhood boss under the Ba'ath Party. Now she styles herself as an ultra-orthodox Shi'ite, shrouded from head to toe in dark funeral clothing, even her chubby little fists concealed in black gloves. The other women at the DAC fear that Fatimah will make the proposed women's center her own private political clubhouse, a place to wield influence and hand out favors to cronies.

With Beta's help, the other DAC women—Jenny, Ahlam and the rest—stage a coup against the grotesque old boss. It comes to a head in a tumultuous meeting: Fatimah, backed by a lone ally, shouts, threatens, interrupts and insults, blaming the U.S. Army for not providing more money, and disparaging her opponents for not being "religious" enough. Finally, elegant, aristocratic Jenny and shy Ahlam have had enough: they more or less tell Fatimah to shut up. The meeting ends with a compromise— Fatimah will stay on as provisional head of the women's group for two months, and then a replacement will be chosen—but over the next few days Beta nudges the anti-Fatimah group to go ahead and dump their nemesis in the next weekly meeting. They proceed to do just that: Fatimah is deposed, and without her interference and obstruction the plans for the women's center go into high gear. Soon there will be sewing and computer classes at the DAC, and seminars in political organizing and fund-raising; guest speakers are going to talk about everything from spousal abuse to child care to how to link up with international women's groups. Around the same time, Beta and the DAC women get exciting news: an NGO based in the Green Zone has come up with over $2 million in funding for women's projects in the Baghdad area, and al-Khadimiyah will get a share of it. When I congratulate Beta for the great job she has done, she claims she didn't do much of anything: "It was all Jenny and her friends," she says. "They did it all. All I did was open up a crack in the door for them, and they went through it."

No wonder the women here love Beta so much; and it's not only in al-Khadimiyah—her reputation has spread beyond the DAC and the surrounding neighborhood. One Baghdad high-school girl regularly e-mails her for advice on her studies, social life, family, fashions, reading, even though the two have never actually met. The affection is not one-sided: a couple of times Beta has told me she would like to return to Iraq someday as a civilian and continue to work with the women here.

And then there are the new English classes, which turn out to be about much more than vocabulary and grammar.

One day Ahlam comes to Sergeant Paul and me and asks us if we could teach a conversational English class at the DAC. We both tell her we would be glad to do it.

Around a week later the first class meets, in one of the offices in the future women's center. The class was originally supposed to be for Ahlam and her friends on the women's committee—they were particularly interested in learning political terminology, to help them confer with non-Iraqis about their plans to encourage democratization—but three of the six women who show up are not committee members, just locals who heard about the class and thought it sounded interesting; and there are five men as well, including one of the chief administrators from the DG office.

It also turns out that the Iraqis are less interested in practicing their English than they are in just sitting and talking informally, no holds barred, with a representative of the American occupation forces. "Interested" does not really do justice to their emotional intensity: I quickly realize these people are desperate, famished, for communication, to express themselves openly, to unburden themselves of all the fears, hopes, resentments and frustrations that have been building up since the very beginning of the occupation. I tell them they can talk about any subject, ask any question and say anything they want. "Feel free," I tell them. "Don't be afraid you're going to make me angry or insult me. I want you to say what you really think." There is a moment of hesitation as they glance at each other; a couple of them smile, one man chuckles, and then they cut loose.

I wish there were a direct line from this cramped little meeting room to Washington, D.C., to the Pentagon, NSC, CIA, Foggy Bottom and the Oval Office. One young Shi'a woman in particular nearly explodes with passion and eloquence: "Why don't you let us choose our own leaders? Who are these people you want us to choose from in these elections of yours? We've never heard of them, we don't know them!" She is smiling as she says all this, but her eyes are flashing like black lasers; she looks like she is about to burst into flames.

"Do you like any of the Iraqi politicians working with the Americans?" I ask.

The whole room erupts with shouts of "No!", laughter, comments between individual Iraqis.

When the noise dies down, I ask another question: "How many of you voted in the last elections?" I'm referring to the balloting the week before for interim representatives.

"No one voted!" The fiery young woman laughs, and there is a chorus of agreement. "Nobody in Khadimiyah voted!" "Why should we Iraqis vote? This is an American election! *You* should vote, not us!" They aren't angry at me or anything like that; the scene is more like the call and response of a preacher and his congregation at a Holy Pentecostal church.

The middle-aged DG administrator tries to sound a quieter, more reasoned note, something conciliatory about how not all the pro-American Iraqi politicians are totally bad, but I find myself reflexively siding with the others: I ask the fiery one to explain why she has so little faith in the Interim Government and its leaders.

"You don't listen to us," she says. "No one listens to us. It was the same under Saddam, and now you Americans and your Iraqi friends are living in Saddam's palaces, and still we have no voice. How can I be heard? How can I tell you what I think, what I want?"

I can't help but smile. "Isn't that what you are doing right now?"

The other Iraqis laugh at this, and to her credit she joins in. "Yes, and it is very good. This is what we need, to be able to talk and have you Americans listen!"

A quiet-looking young man speaks up. "I tell you, when you Americans first came to Iraq, most of us were very happy. We believed you when you said you came to give us our freedom. But now we don't believe you so much anymore. We keep waiting, but all we get is more promises."

"I understand," I tell him. "And I agree, we Americans made a lot of mistakes in Iraq. But don't think that because we do wrong things, bad things, it's because we are bad people. Maybe we are just stupid—maybe we've done bad things here because we didn't know any better."

Another man laughs knowingly, shaking his head. "You

Americans are the only superpower in the world. You can do anything. We don't believe you are stupid." He's not buying ignorance as an excuse; like almost all Iraqis, he thinks every American action, no matter how strange or destructive, is part of some grand, fiendishly clever master plan for global domination. "We know you are very, very smart."

"Well, you're wrong. Just because a country is strong doesn't mean it's wise; you can become so strong you get lazy and don't use your brain anymore, you don't think it's necessary. If we're so intelligent, then why are we in so much trouble here in Iraq? If you could see some of the idiots we have running things in the Green Zone, you'd believe me one hundred percent."

Over the following weeks, the Iraqis talk with Sergeant Paul and me about Christianity and Islam, Israel and Palestine, Sunni and Shi'a Islam, al-Sadr and al-Sistani, war and peace, material progress versus decaying spiritual values. I wonder where else in Iraq Americans and Iraqis are talking to each other this way, telling each other what is really on their minds.

So much of CAT-A 13's success story in al-Khadimiyah is about these seemingly casual contacts between team members and local Iraqis: bargaining for fruit and vegetables at the farm stands beyond the Baghdad Gate, telling the baker opposite the Hurriyah DAC he has the best bread in all of Baghdad, holding up traffic so an old Shi'a lady can cross the busy street by the Begging Poet statue, talking about the things that concern both Iraqis and Americans . . . strangers and enemies turned into neighbors and friends through the most common everyday encounters.

The team has been shopping regularly in the crowded streets near the shrine, buying everything from kitchen appliances to lumber for Kramer's remodeling projects to furniture. It is a neighborhood we have never really been sure of; everyone from CAT-A 13 is on extra alert there, watching the people, the alleyways and rooftops for signs of trouble. One day we have just finished picking up some necessities for the team house and are driving away when Kramer and I see a shifty-looking boy pick up a stone, step out from the crowd and heave it at us. His aim is terrible and the missile falls way short, but the reaction of the Iraqis around him is what really makes us laugh: they shout profanities at the stone thrower, and then they take off after him, led by a fierce old man with an enormous beard. The last we see of the little villain he is running like Iblis himself is on his tail, and the crowd is gaining on him; the old man has grabbed himself a big stick somewhere and is preparing to bring it down on his head.

The team gets a new interpreter, a slender young sapling of a girl named Ayat. Her name, she tells us, means "Dream."

Like so many Iraqi Shi'a women, she is independent, free-spirited and outspoken, and she takes an extremely dim view of Iraqi men and the relationship between the sexes here. Her first morning she arrives at the team house and announces, "I took the bus to work this morning, and all the workmen on board stared at me. I don't like it. Why do they stare? Are they stupid? It's not like that in Syria, Egypt or Lebanon; friends of mine have visited there and they told me. The men here get afraid if a woman gets educated.

"I would never marry an Iraqi man. Most husbands in Iraq hit their wives. They treat them like animals. A man can have three or four wives—it's disgusting!" The words keep tumbling out, like she has so much to say she can't waste time between thoughts. "My mother says Iraqi men have all turned into camels, from living in this desert so long. I don't know why our grandfathers and their fathers came here to live—such an awful place!" She wrinkles her nose disdainfully.

"They must have been really hard workers," I offer, feeling I should try to defend Iraq. I don't know why.

"No, I think they were really stupid," Ayat says.

But when I ask her if she wants to leave Iraq and study or work in Western Europe or the States, she shakes her head adamantly. "No. I don't want to leave Iraq." She is determined to stay, even if the struggle is seemingly hopeless; giving up is apparently not an option.

Women like Ayat, Jenny, Ahlam and their friends will be the salvation of Iraq, assuming Iraq survives. They despise fundamentalists, terrorists and corrupt politicians, any Iraqi who doesn't put his or her country first; their visions of the future are sky-high and diamond-bright, pure, clean and uncompromising. It is nice to think that the soldiers from CAT-A 13 have helped give those visions strength and substance.

15

ON MY LAST ride out to BIAP, to fly home, the Iraqis we pass are still smiling, waving, giving us the thumbs-up of approval, just as they did when I first arrived here in February. And yesterday at the DAC an Iraqi expatriate visiting from one of the Gulf Emirates laughed as he told us, "You know, we Iraqis are really lucky. The Saudis and Kuwaitis had to pay you one hundred billion dollars to save them from Saddam, but you did it for us for free!"

We haven't lost the trust and goodwill of the Iraqi people; not all of it, not yet.

And help is beginning to trickle in from outside, slowly but perceptibly. CAT-A 13 was driving through al-Shula two days ago when we ran into a team of Iraqis by an open manhole, checking out a blocked sewer line. We stopped to talk with them, and it turned out they were working for a European NGO which is planning to do a complete overhaul of the al-Khadimiyah wastewater system; they are even going to replace the local pumping stations with new ones. Another aid group is preparing to build a new pipeline into Sobiabora, furnishing the town with an abundant supply of drinking water for the first time. An Iraqi woman from yet another international NGO, an elegant-looking ash blonde invariably dressed like she is on Fifth Avenue in New

York, has been showing up at the DAC, with an attaché case full
of plans and the money to pay for them.

A new Internet cafe just appeared on the main road through
al-Khadimiyah, a few blocks up from the DAC; throngs of local
teenagers surge in and out the door all day and into the night,
talking with people all over the planet, accessing worlds they
never imagined before. Maybe they are rapping with the ghost of
Qtub, or yukking it up with bin L. in a secret chat room beneath
the floorboards of moslemseekinglory.org; on the other hand,
perhaps they are downloading the lost sessions of the Thomp-
son Twins, cheering on Man United over Liverpool, or scoping
out Bikini Babes of the Big Ten.

This is the road to the Iraq of tomorrow, and medieval pipe
dreams are only one of a hundred million possible destinations.

When you look at what Major Clark and his team have done
here, it may not look like much: green grass and benches around
a couple of traffic circles, clearing of trash, a few hardscrabble
playgrounds and soccer fields, a half dozen committees of
earnest Iraqi citizens trying to cobble together a freer, sweeter
future for themselves.

The innocent security guards accused of wounding the Iraqi
soldier never did get retried and acquitted, but they have taken
advantage of the series of delays by bonding out and bolting,
probably to Syria or Jordan. When justice wasn't served, they
grabbed it and ran.

The monument to the Ashura bombing martyrs still hasn't
been built: Major Clark surmises that someone in a key position
at the DAC wanted his palm greased. (A monument is only

bronze and stone; the fact that Major Clark wanted the dead honored, and that the living saw this for themselves, is in its own way a far more grand and enduring memorial.)

But something really important happened here in al-Khadimiyah: a group of American soldiers met face to face with a neighborhood of Iraqi Shi'a Moslems, and over the course of ten months they discovered they were above all else human beings, who laughed at the same pratfalls and absurdities, cursed at the fickleness of fate and the random injustices of existence, and shared the same dreams. Nowadays when the people of al-Khadimiyah look at the CAT-A 13 soldiers, they no longer see enemies, invaders, strangers: Major Clark and his team have become part of the scenery, boys in the 'hood, the *shebab* from across the seas. "Hey, who're those guys in the Humvees?" "Them? Oh, that's just our local Americans. They're always cruising around trying to fix everything. They're kind of crazy, but they're okay."

Kramer has one last surprise in him. For the last couple of weeks he has been on the computer for hours every night, asking Sergeant Paul, Beta and Espi for technical advice, then going back to work while everyone else is asleep.

One day he proudly produces the fruit of his efforts: a CD-ROM, of pictures he has taken of Iraqi children, set to Louis Armstrong's "What a Wonderful World." He has picked out photos that are particularly heartwarming: a man holding up his baby proudly for the soldiers to admire, a row of angelic little girls smiling shyly, a scamp of a boy grinning, giving the thumbs-up. Everyone, including me, gets a copy, but Kramer tells us he really made tt for his own children back home in Missouri: "I want them to see what it's like over here, that there are kids just like them."

Haifa Street is still Condition Red, and so, in reality, is everything here. Two days ago we visited the Green Zone, and saw Iraqi President Alawi traveling about a mile, from his fortess home to a cabinet meeting inside the Green Zone: there were seven armored vehicles full of bodyguards with him, two helicopters flew cover overhead, and INGs were stationed every fifty feet along his route.

And the last time I was in the Green Zone, Major Pilot, Colonel Lattamore and I were driving around when we noticed a young Iraqi man, a surveyor's compass in his hand, counting off the paces between key buildings. When we questioned him, he claimed someone had given him a compass with a "faulty bubble" and he was testing it. Lattamore checked his ID—he was an interpreter for Titan, the big subcontracting firm—and that night he went to the Titan offices and reported the incident: it looked an awful lot like the interpreter had been pacing out targets for mortar attacks.

"Oh, yeah," the Titan man reportedly told him. "Half our interpreters are working for the other side, but they're all we can get. It's either them or nobody."

32

I AM STILL convinced we can salvage Iraq, and along with it ourselves, our national honor and our traditions of decency and
generosity. If a handful of American soldiers did it here in al-
Khadimiyah, practically on their own, against all odds, then the
same potential is there all across Iraq. The day before I leave
Baghdad, I sit down with a pen and paper and start making a list.
I call it "Seven Ways We Can Save Iraq (and the rest of the
world)," and it reads like this:

1. RECRUIT TEN TIMES AS MANY CIVIL AFFAIRS SOLDIERS. IF
   THAT'S NOT ENOUGH, RECRUIT EVEN MORE.
2. GREATLY INCREASE PAY AND BENEFITS FOR EVERYONE IN
   THE MILITARY, INCLUDING CA. AN ALL-VOLUNTEER ARMY
   HAS TO BE ABLE TO COMPETE WITH THE PRIVATE JOB MAR-
   KET IF IT IS GOING TO ATTRACT THE SKILLED, MOTIVATED
   PEOPLE IT NEEDS.
3. ESTABLISH A CIVIL AFFAIRS MILITARY ACADEMY, ALONG THE
   LINES OF WEST POINT AND ANNAPOLIS, TO TRAIN A WHOLE
   SOVEREIGN CORPS OF SOLDIERS AND MARINES SPECIALIZ-
   ING IN CA, UNDER ITS OWN INDEPENDENT COMMAND.

4. Combine CA troops with Special Forces soldiers and civilian aid workers into self-sufficient nation-building teams strong enough to defend themselves wherever they are sent. (Something like that is being tried in Afghanistan, and it seems to be working. These hybrid units are called PRT's, Provincial Redevelopment Teams, each one with about fifty members.)

5. Stop trying to pretend we're not at war. Open up press offices at BIAP and Camp Victory and the Green Zone, to help make sure the American public knows what we are doing in Iraq and is emotionally involved in it. Sure, some negative stories will get out, but if we're doing the right thing in Iraq, the great majority of the reporting will reflect that fact.

6. Start teaching American soldiers Arabic before they go over to Iraq. We've been occupying the place for nearly two years now and we still have hardly anyone there who can speak the language. In fact, get together with colleges and universities and start teaching Middle Eastern history, Islamic studies and Arab culture to soldiers and non-soldiers alike. Whether we are going to save the world, re-make it or police it, we need to understand it.

7. Triple the overall number of troops in Iraq until real security has been assured. You can't build a nation when you're being blown up or shot in the back.

I thought about it for a while, and then I added this:

8. What we need in Iraq is a lot more CAT-A 13s and Major Clarks.

Everything changes once people get to know each other, just as nothing changes if they don't. The former has happened here in al-Khadimiyah: the people of al-Khadimiyah have had their hearts and minds opened, their world and their future expanded, and there is no going back. No matter what happens in the rest of Iraq, Major Clark and CAT-A 13 have won that part of their little war; and that dusty slice of old Baghdad, on the left bank of the Tigris River, will never be the same again.

AFTERWORD

THREE OR FOUR months after the 425th returned home, a friend of mine in the battalion e-mailed me with news: Major Clark and Sergeant Paul have decided to return to Iraq with the next deployment of CA troops; they hope to go back to al-Khadimiyah. At least one of the other CAT-A 13 members, Shane Cruddas, wants to go with them. So I e-mailed Sergeant Paul, who is at the Army Language School in Monterey, studying—Army logic at work again—Korean:

"Heard you and the Major are headed back to Khadimiyah with another team.

"Think you'll have room on board for a writer?"

ACKNOWLEDGMENTS

WAGING PEACE WOULD not have been possible without the contributions of many people.

First of all, thanks to my wife, Nancy, who kept the home fires burning during all of my journeys to Afghanistan, Iraq, and other troubled places. My mother and brother in Virginia provided nonstop support during the researching and writing of the book, plus the hospitality of the family home back east when I was meeting with sources in the Washington, D.C., area.

Col. Roger Walker and the members of the Chiclet-5 gave me my first look at Civil Affairs in action, and their superb work in Bamiyan inspired me to pursue the CA story in depth. Without *Time* magazine editor Howard Hsua-eng's enthusiastic backing of the Bamiyan story, I would have had a difficult if not impossible time doing the initial journalistic groundwork on CA.

My agent, Scott Gold, and the rest of the people at Zachary Shuster Harmsworth worked tirelessly helping me write the book proposal that made *Waging Peace* a reality. By placing the book with Brendan Cahill at Gotham Books, Scott put me together with the best editor I could have wished for; Brendan's shaping of the book's flow and his keen eye for narrative precision throughout helped immeasurably in doing justice to the story of CAT-A 13 and the U.S. Army Civil Affairs as a whole.

I owe a very special debt of gratitude to Gen. Dennis Wilkie (Ret.), the leading spokesperson for both Civil Affairs veterans and active duty CA soldiers, for steering me through the long, fascinating history of Civil Affairs in the U.S. military and the challenges facing it today. It is fair to say that everything I know about CA is due to General Wilkie's generous efforts.

Civil Affairs soldiers past and present, men like Col. Robert Frame and Col. Herman Frankel, shared their wartime experiences with me; it was a privilege and an honor to talk with them, and to bring their stories to the public at large.

At Fort Bragg, Ben Abel of the USACAPOC press office and Gen. Herbert Altschuler, commanding officer of the USACAPOC, opened up the doors to the Civil Affairs mission in Iraq for me. In doing so, they trusted me to tell the story fairly and accurately, and I hope I haven't disappointed them. If I have, it isn't for lack of trying to "tell it right."

In Iraq, thanks to Lt. Col. Sean Kelly of the 425th CA Battalion, and all the good friends I made in the 425th, for everything; especially Maj. John Pilot, Col. Oliver Lattamore, Sgt. Bob Venters, and Sgt. Maj. Church, though I am inevitably leaving out some names. Thanks also to my 1/5 Cav and Iraq friends.

And, of course, to Maj. Mark Clark and everyone in CAT-A 13: "I've got your back."